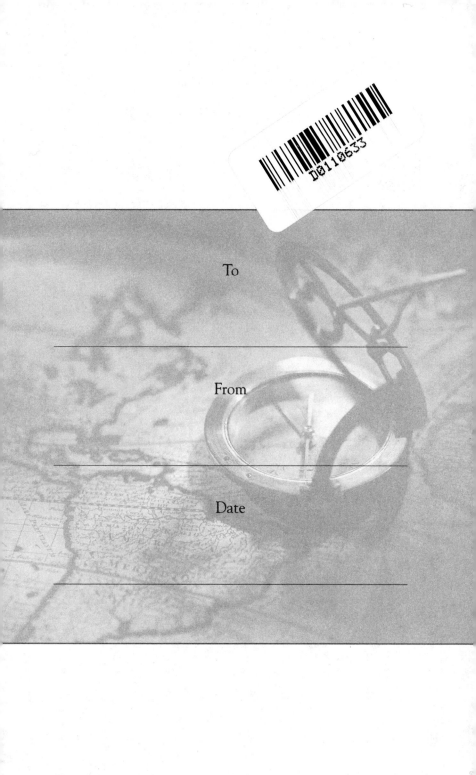

To

From

Date

ABOVE ALL ELSE
Directions for life

*Above all else, guard your heart, for it
affects everything you do.*
Proverbs 4:23-27 NLT

DR. CRISWELL FREEMAN
WITH TIM WAY

Scripture quotations are taken from:

The Holy Bible, King James Version

The Holy Bible, New International Version (NIV) Copyright © 1973, 1978, 1984, by International Bible Society. Used by permission of Zondervan Publishing House. All rights reserved.

The New American Standard Bible®, (NASB) Copyright © 1960, 1962, 1963, 1968, 1971, 1972, 1973, 1975, 1977, 1995 by The Lockman Foundation. Used by permission.

The Holy Bible, New King James Version (NKJV) Copyright © 1982 by Thomas Nelson, Inc. Used by permission.

The Holy Bible, New Living Translation, (NLT) Copyright © 1996. Used by permission of Tyndale House Publishers, Inc., Wheaton, Illinois 60189. All rights reserved.

New Century Version®. (NCV) Copyright © 1987, 1988, 1991 by Word Publishing, a division of Thomas Nelson, Inc. All rights reserved. Used by permission.

The Holy Bible: Revised Standard Version (RSV). Copyright 1946, 1952, 1959, 1973 by the Division of Christian Education of the National Council of the Churches of Christ in the United States of America. All rights reserved. Used by permission.

The Holy Bible, The Living Bible (TLB), Copyright © 1971 owned by assignment by Illinois Regional Bank N.A. (as trustee). Used by permission of Tyndale House Publishers, Inc., Wheaton, Illinois 60189. All rights reserved.

The Message (MSG) This edition issued by contractual arrangement with NavPress, a division of The Navigators, U.S.A. Originally published by NavPress in English as THE MESSAGE: The Bible in Contemporary Language copyright 2002-2003 by Eugene Peterson. All rights reserved.

The Holman Christian Standard Bible™ (HOLMAN CSB) Copyright © 1999, 2000, 2001 by Holman Bible Publishers. Used by permission.

Cover Design by Kim Russell / Wahoo Designs
Page Layout by Bart Dawson

ISBN 1-58334-367-9

ABOVE ALL ELSE
Directions for life

DR. CRISWELL FREEMAN
WITH TIM WAY

TABLE OF CONTENTS

Above all else, guard your heart, for it
affects everything you do. Avoid all perverse talk;
stay far from corrupt speech. Look straight ahead,
and fix your eyes on what lies before you.
Mark out a straight path for your feet; then
stick to the path and stay safe. Don't get sidetracked;
keep your feet from following evil.

Proverbs 4:23-27 NLT

ABOVE ALL ELSE . . .

A PARABLE BY TIM WAY

To the casual observer, the old man might have appeared to be dead. He had sat slumped in the large chair for the past three hours—his chin resting on his chest, eyes closed. Every now and then, his eyelids would twitch, or a soft sigh would escape his throat, but other than that, he was perfectly still. An undignified stream of drool had slowly rolled from one corner of his mouth and run into his white beard.

King Solomon was asleep.

The harsh sound of pottery smashing against a wall suddenly interrupted his peace. It was not close, mind you, but close enough to filter into his subconscious and bring him into that foggy place between sleep and wakefulness. For several minutes, he drifted back and forth.

When he'd earlier let weariness overtake him, it was just after noon. Now through half-closed eyelids, he could see that the late afternoon sun pierced through the western windows of the large study at a sharp angle, sending shafts of light through the latticework in the two narrow openings. The brightness made bold geometric patterns on the floor. He sat for some time contemplating the flecks of dust floating in the hazy glow, watching the patterns of light in their almost imperceptible march across the room.

He raised his head. "I love this place," he thought as he looked around. Of all the private rooms in his palace, this study was his favorite—a place he visited often. Now in the later part of his reign, he came here almost daily. Some days he came to

escape the grueling pace of palace life, some days to write, and
some days just to think or take a nap. Most would consider this
sitting and watching and thinking a waste of time, but he did
not. Sitting, watching, and thinking had been the genesis of
numerous revelations.

"What woke me?" he muttered. "No, not you," he said as he
looked down at the large, sleeping dog whose gray muzzle rested
on his feet. No one else in his kingdom dared assume such an
intimate closeness. "You're almost as ancient as me, old girl,"
the old king chuckled as he reached to scratch the dog's shaggy
head.

Then he heard it again—crashing pottery followed by angry
voices coming from the women's chambers. He moaned. "Not
again. Why can't they get along? I should have stopped with
only one. What made me think that seven hundred wives could
exist peacefully with each other? They are like the constant
dripping of water, wearing me down little by little. And there
are hundreds of them, always nagging, whining, shouting
and yapping like a bunch of spoiled children from sunup to
sundown." He put his head in his hands and sighed deeply.

While he only kept fifty or so of his most favored wives at
the main palace, even that was no guarantee that they would
not become violent with each other. Some did not even speak
his language, and some he had only seen on their wedding day.
Most of them he had married as a part of what he considered the
cost of keeping peace with his neighbors. "And they are quite a
cost," he thought. "They have cost me peace of mind and a part
of my soul." He was so much closer to Yahweh before all of this
marrying and accumulation of wealth.

The king's study was a perfect square—the top story of a
tower sitting in the middle of the palace wall, extending four

stories up from the ground. The tower's western wall formed a part of the outer wall of the palace. There were windows on all sides—two on each wall. The eastern windows overlooked a large courtyard in the interior of the palace. The courtyard, over three hundred square feet, was surrounded on three sides by the palace's interior buildings, and on the west by the outer wall and the tower. The western windows looked out over one of the busiest streets in Jerusalem. Here, people moved about in their daily routines, unaware that they were often being observed by the king. The north and south windows of the tower room looked down each length of the western palace wall. To the south, he could see the walls of the great temple with the Holy Place extending toward the heavens. The walls of the Holy Place were trimmed in pure gold and gleamed in the setting spring sun. Of all his accomplishments, the Temple of Yahweh was his most prized.

Two of his soldiers could be seen moving along the palace wall on patrol. They were dressed in the crisp blue and white dress uniform of the palace guard. Each carried a polished bronze shield that was a replica of the pure gold shields hanging in the great ceremonial hall, and their spears were tipped with genuine silver. His soldiers were not there because of any known threats to the kingdom, but because prudence demanded that they remain on guard. Besides, the palace walls were three stories high and the entire complex stood as a virtual fortress in the middle of one of the most fortified cities in the world.

The study's stone walls were lined with fragrant cedar from Lebanon. Even though the paneling had been installed fifteen years prior, it still had a sweet fragrance that greeted visitors to the room. Tapestries of incomparable value hung over the paneling—gifts from kings in surrounding countries.

The furniture was heavy and finely carved, most of it built for appearance rather than comfort. But the chair in which the king sat was designed specifically for his rather stout frame. Its perfect fit and thick padding, along with a built-in footrest made this the perfect place for thinking—and sleeping.

The room was not originally intended to be a private study. It was actually built as a part of the defensive aspects of the palace, but because of the extended peace, it was not needed for that purpose. So, the king had long ago claimed it as his personal study—a private sanctuary and his place to write letters, proverbs and poetry. The perfect view of the city and the temple, and the solitude it provided, made this simple room the king's most favorite spot on earth.

Solomon sat for another twenty minutes watching the sun's slow march across the stone floor. It was approaching twilight. Reaching for the wine goblet, he snorted in frustration when he found it empty. He was about to ring the bell to summon a servant when he heard voices filtering up from the street below.

"Here they are again," he said to the dog. Grunting loudly, he pulled himself up out of the chair and shuffled across to the window, the dog following closely but lazily at his heels.

Looking down through the ornate lattice work to the street below, he watched a group of young men in their late teens standing together. They were noisy and brash with a cockiness that came from inexperience and youth. Their voices were far too loud, and even though it was early evening, they were well on their way to being drunk. Their bragging about yet unaccomplished exploits only enhanced their foolishness. If they were trying to impress the palace guards looking down from the wall, they were wasting their time. Real men like his soldiers were only mildly amused by boys pretending to be men.

He had observed them here before. They frequented a tavern two streets over, and were just beginning to discover the joys of wasting their fathers' money on wine and who knows what all else.

The king shook his head. "If only they realized how utterly foolish they sound!" He was glad that his son, Rehoboam, was not a part of this group. "But only because I won't let him. If I gave him half a chance he would be down there with them. No, on second thought, he would be down there leading them in their folly," he thought.

The group began to move up the street to his right. One young man, however, hung back. "Hey, Judah, are you coming with us?" they called out to him.

"Uh, no. Not right now. You go on ahead. Maybe I'll catch up later. The usual place?" Judah replied, glancing over his shoulder as he spoke.

"Okay. Sure. Your loss!" they shouted back as they walked away.

"Maybe there is hope for this one," the old king thought. But then he looked up the street to his left and saw her. She was slowly pacing back and forth at the head of the lane. He had seen her before. She was in her late twenties; the only wife of an old wealthy merchant who often left Jerusalem to travel to Lebanon and beyond in search of wares to sell in his shop. She had married him not for love, but for his money. Now, as she often did when left by herself, she had painted her face and had traded her everyday clothes for a costume more suited to her true nature. Her clothes were clearly intended to attract the men that visited this street in search for a companion for the night—for a price. Here, on the other side of the city from her home, she could pretend to be someone else, luring men into a squalid rented room that she paid for from the profits of her part-time trade.

What motivated her to act like a prostitute? Was it the money? Not likely. Her husband gave her anything she wanted. Was it the excitement or the need to feel desired? No one aside from her and Yahweh would ever know.

The young man had seen this woman standing on this corner before and had determined that he would one day work up enough courage to approach her. For a price, he knew that he could have her for the evening, even though under normal circumstances, she would not give his young face a second glance.

She stood with her hands on her hips, watching him approach. His steps were a little unsteady, betraying his inability to handle his wine. He was trying his best to act nonchalant, but was unsuccessful in the attempt. Glancing nervously this way and that, he was obviously trying to assure that his father or one of his father's associates was not watching. When he was about five feet away from her, she shocked him by running up, boldly taking his face in her hands, and kissing him full on the mouth.

"Stop!" the king cried out. "You fool!" For a moment Judah hesitated. What was that he had just heard? He looked nervously behind him. Seeing no one, he gave his attention back to the woman.

She threw her head back and laughed loudly. "Come with me, my love. I have the makings of a feast—today I made my offerings, my vows are all paid!" The sound of her voice carried from the street up to the tower window.

"This woman is fit only for stoning," the king muttered to himself. "Moses and my father David would not have put up with this foolishness. Why have we gone so far astray from the ancient ways? The very nerve this woman has—to bring the things of God into this sinful act!"

The young man looked frantically around him. He had not expected her to be so bold or so loud. He was beginning to regret his decision. Besides, she did not look as good up close as she did from the other end of the street, and her breath smelled of stale wine.

"So now I've come to find you, hoping to catch sight of your face—and here you are!" she continued loudly.

"You liar!" thought the king. "You would have latched onto the first idiot that came down the street with money in his pocket."

Putting her arms around the young man and pulling him close, she purred, "Come, my love. I've spread fresh, clean sheets on my bed, colorful imported linens. My bed is covered with spices and exotic fragrances. Come! Let's make love all night and spend the night in ecstatic lovemaking! My husband's not home. He's away on business and he won't be back for a month."

With that, she put her arm through the young man's, and steered him down the street like a sheep going to slaughter, laughing loudly as she led him out of sight.

"If her husband finds out who has been sleeping with her while he is gone, he will have one of his servants cut out this young fool's heart and throw it to his dogs," the king thought. He was suddenly overcome with a great sadness—for the young man and for all of the young men in his nation. "Why, oh why, my Lord, do they behave so foolishly? Why do they act in this manner?"

While he hadn't actually expected an answer, one came clearly and immediately. The sudden impact almost drove him to his knees.

"It is because they have such poor example as a king," the Spirit spoke. "It is because the spiritual fervor has left your kingdom and has been replaced by a shallow, token nod to me, Yahweh, in the midst of obscene materialism. I have blessed you, but you have squandered my blessings by forgetting me!"

Solomon slowly sank into the chair at the desk. Holding his head in his hands, he slowly rocked back and forth as he let the words from the Spirit sink deep into his soul. His mind drifted back over the years of his reign. What promise! What blessings! Now, nothing was left but regrets and broken potential. He had more wealth than he could count, yet he was miserable. His people were wandering further and further away from Yahweh. How could so much be right, and yet everything be so wrong? Oh, for the smile of Yahweh once again!

Solomon sighed as he picked up the quill lying on the desk and dipped it in the inkwell. It had been a long time since he had felt the Spirit stirring in him. Years of self indulgence had dulled the moving of Yahweh on his soul, and the occurrences of divine inspiration on his writing had all but stopped. Today, however, was different. The Spirit's moving had started long before dawn and had continued into the noon hour. The words seemed to spill out of him onto the parchment. It was like years ago, when he regularly felt Yahweh's tug on his heart.

He looked at the last words he had written in the hours before his nap. His thoughts were of his son, Rehoboam, the one that would likely inherit the kingdom. "The boy is brash and foolish," he thought. "He speaks without thinking. Without my strong hand on his backside he would be out on the street with those other drunken fools. He listens to no one but the young men that surround him—young pups of privilege who are totally out of touch with the people. How will he govern a people he does not even understand or care about? Oh, if only he were more like his grandfather, David. I fear for the people of Israel when I go to be with my fathers."

Early that morning, Solomon had walked up the flight of stairs to the tower room and sat in this very spot watching the sun rise over the palace buildings. The Spirit had stirred deeply on his soul and he had written, "*The path of the righteous is like the first gleam of dawn, shining ever brighter till the full light of day. But the way of the wicked is like deep darkness; they do not know what makes them stumble.*"

His thoughts went back to the young man on the street. "This could apply fully to him," the king thought. "He is stumbling around in the dark and will end up in a hole that will destroy him."

His thoughts went to his own son. As he began to write, he could feel the stirring once again of the Spirit and his pen moved urgently across the parchment.

"*My son, pay attention to what I say; listen closely to my words. Do not let them out of your sight, keep them within your heart; for they are life to those who find them and health to a man's whole body.*"

Where had he gone wrong? What were the early signs that he was going the wrong direction? His heart had once burned hot for Jehovah. He thought back to the dedication of the temple and that awesome time when the presence of God filled the Holy of Holies on that dedication day. What an experience!

Then there was God's promise to bless him when he chose wisdom over riches. And the blessings that had poured in on him were more than he could have ever imagined in his wildest dreams. He had riches, power, wisdom—success at every turn.

But something happened. Maybe it was the great success.

Maybe it was the ease with which wealth came his way. Maybe it was the many wives. He could justify them by saying they were necessary to make alliances, but the fact was that Jehovah had said not to take many wives. The end result was that his heart had grown cold—almost dead.

So, he threw himself into every pursuit he could imagine; intellectual pursuits, money, power, science, and building projects. None of them brought any satisfaction. All of it was pure vanity.

He turned his eyes back to the parchment in front of him. The Spirit's warmth washed over his body, and almost as if his hand took on a life of its own, he wrote again.

"Above all else, guard your heart, for it is the wellspring of life."

"That's it!" he almost shouted. "I have let down my guard and deceived my heart."

"What should I have done, my Lord?" he whispered. The Spirit whispered back the answer softly through his soul. Tears began to course down his wrinkled face, as his quill touched the paper once again.

"Put away perversity from your mouth; keep corrupt talk far from your lips. Let your eyes look straight ahead, fix your gaze directly before you. Make level paths for your feet and take only ways that are firm. Do not swerve to the right or the left; keep your foot from evil."

Through his tears, the old king looked at what he had just written. "My God, I repent before you," he said as he fell to his old knees and wept. "I will take a spotless lamb to your temple when the sun rises in the morning, and make a proper sacrifice for my sins. Forgive me, Yahweh, for letting down the guard on my heart, for speaking in ways that displease you, for looking and coveting what was not really mine to own, and most of all, for taking paths that were not firm. It is too late for me. I have been a poor example to my sons and my nation. I fear the price they will pay for my sins. Be gracious to them, my God."

The sun had set and darkness had settled over the palace when the old king finally rose slowly and stiffly to his feet. He rang the bell for his servant. He would have something sent up from the kitchen to eat. Something simple.

Even though nothing had really changed, he suddenly felt lighter. Though the urging of the Spirit had lifted, he knew that he had probably just written the most important words of his life. He would give them to his son. Would he listen? Probably not, but he would try anyway. If not Rehoboam, then perhaps someone else in the future would benefit from the words given to him that day by Jehovah.

My son, pay attention to what I say; listen closely to my words.
Do not let them out of your sight, keep them within your heart;
For they are life to those who find them
And health to a man's whole body.
Above all else, guard your heart, for it is the wellspring of life.
Put away perversity from your mouth; keep corrupt talk far from
*   your lips.*
Let your eyes look straight ahead, fix your gaze directly before you.
Make level paths for your feet and take only ways that are firm.
Do not swerve to the right or the left; keep your foot from evil.

Proverbs 4:20–27

While the scene of the young man and the prostitute is fictional, it has basis in fact and can be found in Proverbs 7:6–23.

INTRODUCTION

God's Word is clear: we are to guard our hearts "above all else," yet we live in a world that encourages us to do otherwise. Here in the 21st century, temptations and distractions are woven into the fabric of everyday life. As believers, we must remain vigilant. Not only must we resist Satan when he confronts us, but we must also avoid those places where Satan can most easily tempt us. And, this book is intended to help.

In Proverbs 4:23-27, we are instructed to guard our words, our eyes, and our path. This text examines these instructions through a collection of essays, Bible verses, and quotations from noted Christian men and women.

As a way of introducing these ideas, this book began with a parable by Tim Way—a story about temptation in the ancient city of Jerusalem and about how human waywardness, coupled with divine insight, might have influenced the writings of an aged king. Tim's story is followed by a series of practical lessons, lessons about protecting ourselves against the trials and temptations that have become inescapable elements of modern-day life.

Each day, you must make countless choices that can bring you closer to God, or not. When you guard your heart—and when you live in accordance with God's commandments—you will inevitably earn His blessings. But if you make unwise choices, or if you yield to the temptations of this difficult age, you must pay a price for your shortsightedness, perhaps a very high price.

Would you like to avoid the dangers and temptations that Satan will inevitably place along your path? And would you like to experience God's peace and His abundance? Then guard your heart above all else. When you're tempted to speak an unkind word, hold your tongue. When you're faced with a difficult choice or a powerful temptation, seek God's counsel and trust the counsel He gives. When you're uncertain of your next step, follow in the footsteps of God's only begotten Son. Invite God into your heart and live according to His commandments. When you do, you will be blessed today, tomorrow, and forever.

PART 1

GUARD
YOUR WORDS

GUARD YOUR SPEECH

*We all make many mistakes, but those who control their tongues
can also control themselves in every other way.*

James 3:2 NLT

The words that we speak have great power. If our words
are encouraging, we can lift others up; if our words are
hurtful, we can hold others back. The Bible reminds us
that "Reckless words pierce like a sword, but the tongue of the
wise brings healing" (Proverbs 12:18 NIV). Therefore, if we
are to solve more problems than we start, we must measure our
words carefully.

Sometimes, even the most thoughtful among us speak first
and think second (with decidedly mixed results). When we're
frustrated or tired, we may speak words that would be better
left unspoken. Whenever we lash out in anger, we forgo the
wonderful opportunity to consider our thoughts before we give
voice to them.

A far better strategy, of course, is to do the more difficult
thing: to think first and to speak next. When we do so, we give
ourselves ample time to compose our thoughts and to consult
our Creator (but not necessarily in that order!).

The Bible warns us that we will be judged by the words we
speak (Matthew 12:36-37). And, Ephesians 4:29 reminds us that

we can—and should—make "each word a gift." To do otherwise is to invite God's displeasure.

Do you seek to be a source of encouragement to others? Are you a beacon of hope to your friends and family? And, do you seek to be a worthy ambassador for Christ? If so, you must speak words that are worthy of your Savior. So avoid angry outbursts. Refrain from impulsive outpourings. Terminate tantrums. Instead, speak words of encouragement and hope to a world that desperately needs both.

Be gracious in your speech.
The goal is to bring out the best in others
in a conversation, not put them down,
not cut them out.

Colossians 4:6 MSG

A TIP FOR GUARDING YOUR HEART

God understands the importance of the words you speak . . . and so must you.

WORDS OF WISDOM

The things that we feel most deeply we ought to learn to be silent about, at least until we have talked them over thoroughly with God.

Elisabeth Elliot

We will always experience regret when we live for the moment and do not weigh our words and deeds before we give them life.

Lisa Bevere

The great test of a man's character is his tongue.

Oswald Chambers

In all your deeds and words, you should look on Jesus as your model, whether you are keeping silence or speaking, whether you are alone or with others.

St. Bonaventure

If you can't think of something nice to say, keep thinking.

Anonymous

GOD'S WORDS OF WISDOM

Watch the way you talk. Let nothing foul or dirty come out of your mouth. Say only what helps, each word a gift.

Ephesians 4:29 MSG

If anyone considers himself religious and yet does not keep a tight rein on his tongue, he deceives himself and his religion is worthless.

James 1:26 NIV

So then, rid yourselves of all evil, all lying, hypocrisy, jealousy, and evil speech. As newborn babies want milk, you should want the pure and simple teaching. By it you can grow up and be saved.

1 Peter 2:1–2 NCV

To everything there is a season . . . a time to keep silence, and a time to speak.

Ecclesiastes 3:1, 7 KJV

SUMMING IT UP

You can guard your heart by paying careful attention to the words you speak. So measure your words carefully and prayerfully.

GUARD YOUR WORDS BY CELEBRATING LIFE

This is the day the LORD has made; we will rejoice and be glad in it.

Psalm 118:24 NKJV

Today is a non-renewable resource—once it's gone, it's gone forever. Our responsibility, as thoughtful believers, is to use this day in the service of God's will and in the service of His people. When we do so, we enrich our own lives and the lives of those whom we love.

God has richly blessed us, and He wants you to rejoice in His gifts. That's why this day—and each day that follows—should be a time of prayer and celebration as we consider the Good News of God's free gift: salvation through Jesus Christ.

Oswald Chambers correctly observed, "Joy is the great note all throughout the Bible." E. Stanley Jones echoed that thought when he wrote "Christ and joy go together." But, even the most dedicated Christians can, on occasion, forget to celebrate each day for what it is: a priceless gift from God.

What do you expect from the day ahead? Are you expecting God to do wonderful things, or are you living beneath a cloud of apprehension and doubt? The familiar words of Psalm 118:24 remind us of a profound yet simple truth: "This is the day which the LORD hath made" (KJV). Our duty, as believers, is to rejoice in God's marvelous creation.

Today, celebrate the life that God has given you. Today, put a smile on your face, kind words on your lips, and a song in your heart. Be generous with your praise and free with your encouragement. And then, when you have celebrated life to the fullest, invite your friends to do likewise. After all, this is God's day, and He has given us clear instructions for its use. We are commanded to rejoice and be glad. So, with no further ado, let the celebration begin . . .

Delight thyself also in the LORD;
and he shall give thee the desires of thine heart.

Psalm 37:4 KJV

A TIP FOR GUARDING YOUR HEART

Every day should be a cause for celebration. By celebrating the gift of life, you protect your heart from the dangers of pessimism, regret, hopelessness, and bitterness.

Words of Wisdom

If you can forgive the person you were, accept the person you are, and believe in the person you will become, you are headed for joy. So celebrate your life.

Barbara Johnson

Some of us seem so anxious about avoiding hell that we forget to celebrate our journey toward heaven.

Philip Yancey

Life is a glorious opportunity.

Billy Graham

The happiest people in the world are not those who have no problems, but the people who have learned to live with those things that are less than perfect.

James Dobson

Christ is the secret, the source, the substance, the center, and the circumference of all true and lasting gladness.

Mrs. Charles E. Cowman

GOD'S WORDS OF WISDOM

Shout for joy to the LORD, all the earth. Worship the LORD with gladness; come before him with joyful songs.

Psalm 100:1-2 NIV

So now we can rejoice in our wonderful new relationship with God—all because of what our Lord Jesus Christ has done for us in making us friends of God.

Romans 5:11 NLT

David and the whole house of Israel were celebrating with all their might before the LORD, with songs and with harps, lyres, tambourines, sistrums and cymbals.

2 Samuel 6:5 NIV

At the dedication of the wall of Jerusalem, the Levites were sought out from where they lived and were brought to Jerusalem to celebrate joyfully the dedication with songs of thanksgiving and with the music of cymbals, harps and lyres.

Nehemiah 12:27 NIV

SUMMING IT UP

God has given you the gift of life (here on earth) and the promise of eternal life (in heaven). Now, He wants you to celebrate those gifts.

GUARD YOUR WORDS BY BEING GRATEFUL

Give thanks to the Lord, for He is good;
His faithful love endures forever.

Psalm 106:1 Holman CSB

As Christians, we are blessed beyond measure. God sent His only Son to die for our sins. And, God has given us the priceless gifts of eternal love and eternal life. We, in turn, are instructed to approach our Heavenly Father with reverence and thanksgiving. But sometimes, in the crush of everyday living, we simply don't stop long enough to pause and thank our Creator for the countless blessings He has bestowed upon us.

When we slow down and express our gratitude to the One who made us, we enrich our own lives and the lives of those around us. Thanksgiving should become a habit, a regular part of our daily routines. God has blessed us beyond measure, and we owe Him everything, including our eternal praise.

Are you a thankful person? Do you appreciate the gifts that God has given you? And, do you demonstrate your gratitude by being a faithful steward of the gifts and talents that you have received from your Creator? You most certainly should be thankful. After all, when you stop to think about it, God has given you more blessings than you can count. So the question of the day is this: will you thank your Heavenly Father . . . or will you spend your time and energy doing other things?

God is always listening—are you willing to say thanks? It's up to you, and the next move is yours.

I will give You thanks with all my heart.

Psalm 138:1 Holman CSB

A TIP FOR GUARDING YOUR HEART

Don't overlook God's gifts. Every sunrise represents yet another beautifully wrapped gift from God. Unwrap it; treasure it; use it; and give thanks to the Giver.

WORDS OF WISDOM

We give strength to our souls as we train ourselves to speak words of thankfulness and praise.

Annie Chapman

Go outside, to the fields, enjoy nature and the sunshine, go out and try to recapture happiness in yourself and in God. Think of all the beauty that's still left in and around you and be happy!

Anne Frank

The words "thank" and "think" come from the same root word. If we would think more, we would thank more.

Warren Wiersbe

The best way to show my gratitude to God is to accept everything, even my problems, with joy.

Mother Teresa

The unthankful heart discovers no mercies; but the thankful heart will find, in every hour, some heavenly blessings!

Henry Ward Beecher

GOD'S WORDS OF WISDOM

Therefore as you have received Christ Jesus the Lord, walk in Him, rooted and built up in Him and established in the faith, just as you were taught, and overflowing with thankfulness.

Colossians 2:6-7 Holman CSB

Thanks be to God for His indescribable gift.

2 Corinthians 9:15 Holman CSB

Give thanks to the Lord, for He is good; His faithful love endures forever.

Psalm 118:29 Holman CSB

And whatever you do, in word or in deed, do everything in the name of the Lord Jesus, giving thanks to God the Father through Him.

Colossians 3:17 Holman CSB

SUMMING IT UP

By speaking words of thanksgiving and praise, you honor the Father and you protect your heart against the twin evils of apathy and ingratitude.

GUARD YOUR WORDS BY STRIVING TO BE PATIENT

Always be humble, gentle, and patient, accepting each other in love.
Ephesians 4:2 NCV

The dictionary defines the word patience as "the ability to be calm, tolerant, and understanding." If that describes you, you can skip the rest of this page. But, if you're like most of us, you'd better keep reading.

For most of us, patience is a hard thing to master. Why? Because we have lots of things we want, and we know precisely when we want them: NOW (if not sooner). But our Father in heaven has other ideas; the Bible teaches that we must learn to wait patiently for the things that God has in store for us, even when waiting is difficult.

We live in an imperfect world inhabited by imperfect people. Sometimes, we inherit troubles from others, and sometimes we create troubles for ourselves. On other occasions, we see other people "moving ahead" in the world, and we want to move ahead with them. So we become impatient with ourselves, with our circumstances, and even with our Creator.

Psalm 37:7 commands us to "rest in the Lord, and wait patiently for Him" (NKJV). But, for most of us, waiting patiently for Him is hard. We are fallible human beings who seek solutions to our problems today, not tomorrow. Still, God instructs us to wait patiently for His plans to unfold, and that's exactly what we should do.

Sometimes, patience is the price we pay for being responsible adults, and that's as it should be. After all, think about how patient our heavenly Father has been with us. So the next time you find yourself drumming your fingers as you wait for a quick resolution to the challenges of everyday living, take a deep breath and ask God for patience. Be still before your Heavenly Father and trust His timetable: it's the peaceful way to live.

Patience is better than strength.

Proverbs 16:32 ICB

A Tip for Guarding Your Heart

If you want folks to be patient with you, then you must do the same for them. Never expect other people to be more patient with you than you are with them.

WORDS OF WISDOM

Waiting is an essential part of spiritual discipline. It can be the ultimate test of faith.

Anne Graham Lotz

In the Bible, patience is not a passive acceptance of circumstances. It is a courageous perseverance in the face of suffering and difficulty.

Warren Wiersbe

The next time you're disappointed, don't panic. Don't give up. Just be patient and let God remind you he's still in control.

Max Lucado

He makes us wait. He keeps us in the dark on purpose. He makes us walk when we want to run, sit still when we want to walk, for he has things to do in our souls that we are not interested in.

Elisabeth Elliot

When we read of the great Biblical leaders, we see that it was not uncommon for God to ask them to wait, not just a day or two, but for years, until God was ready for them to act.

Gloria Gaither

GOD'S WORDS OF WISDOM

But if we look forward to something we don't have yet, we must wait patiently and confidently.

Romans 8:25 NLT

The Lord is wonderfully good to those who wait for him and seek him. So it is good to wait quietly for salvation from the Lord.

Lamentations 3:25-26 NLT

Wait on the LORD; Be of good courage, and He shall strengthen your heart; Wait, I say, on the LORD!

Psalm 27:14 NKJV

Patience and encouragement come from God. And I pray that God will help you all agree with each other the way Christ Jesus wants.

Romans 15:5 NCV

SUMMING IT UP

When you learn to be more patient with others, you'll make your world—and your heart—a better place.

GUARD YOUR WORDS WITH AN ENTHUSIASTIC HEART

Whatever you do, do it enthusiastically,
as something done for the Lord and not for men.

Colossians 3:23 Holman CSB

Can you truthfully say that you are an enthusiastic believer? Are you passionate about your faith and excited about your path? Hopefully so. But if your zest for life has waned, it is now time to redirect your efforts and recharge your spiritual batteries. And that means refocusing your priorities by putting God first.

Nothing is more important than your wholehearted commitment to your Creator and to His only begotten Son. Your faith must never be an afterthought; it must be your ultimate priority, your ultimate possession, and your ultimate passion. When you become passionate about your faith, you'll become passionate about your life, too.

When the stresses of everyday life seem overwhelming, you may not feel very enthusiastic about your life or yourself. On those difficult days when the pressures of life threaten to overwhelm your passion for life, it's time to reorder your thoughts, your priorities, and your prayers. When you do so, you'll soon discover that genuine, heartfelt enthusiasm is contagious—and so is your enthusiastic testimony of the changes that God has made in your life.

Are you genuinely excited about your faith? And do you make your enthusiasm known to those around you? Or are you satisfied to be a "silent ambassador" for Christ? God's preference is clear: He prefers enthusiasm to apathy, and so should you.

Remember: You are the recipient of Christ's sacrificial love. Accept it enthusiastically and share it passionately. Jesus deserves your enthusiasm; the world deserves it; and you deserve the experience of sharing it.

Never be lazy in your work,
but serve the Lord enthusiastically.

Romans 12:11 NLT

A TIP FOR GUARDING YOUR HEART

Don't wait for enthusiasm to find you . . . go looking for it. Look at your life and your relationships as exciting adventures. Don't wait for life to spice itself; spice things up yourself.

WORDS OF WISDOM

Enthusiasm, like the flu, is contagious—we get it from one another.

Barbara Johnson

There seems to be a chilling fear of holy enthusiasm among the people of God. We try to tell how happy we are—but we remain so well-controlled that there are very few waves of glory experienced in our midst.

A. W. Tozer

One of the great needs in the church today is for every Christian to become enthusiastic about his faith in Jesus Christ.

Billy Graham

We act as though comfort and luxury were the chief requirements of life, when all we need to make us really happy is something to be enthusiastic about.

Charles Kingsley

When we wholeheartedly commit ourselves to God, there is nothing mediocre or run-of-the-mill about us. To live for Christ is to be passionate about our Lord and about our lives.

Jim Gallery

GOD'S WORDS OF WISDOM

Whatever work you do, do your best, because you are going to the grave, where there is no working . . . .

Ecclesiastes 9:10 NCV

I have seen that there is nothing better than for a person to enjoy his activities, because that is his reward. For who can enable him to see what will happen after he dies?

Ecclesiastes 3:22 Holman CSB

Do your work with enthusiasm. Work as if you were serving the Lord, not as if you were serving only men and women.

Ephesians 6:7 NCV

So, my dear brothers and sisters, be strong and steady, always enthusiastic about the Lord's work, for you know that nothing you do for the Lord is ever useless.

1 Corinthians 15:58 NLT

SUMMING IT UP

When you become genuinely enthused about your life and your faith, you'll guard your heart and improve your life.

GUARD YOUR WORDS WITH SILENCE

Be silent before the Lord and wait expectantly for Him.

Psalm 37:7 Holman CSB

Here's a simple prescription for guarding your words and your heart: Carve out a little time for silence every day. Here in our noisy, 21st-century world, silence is highly underrated. Many of us can't even seem to walk from the front door to the street without a cell phone or an iPod in our ear. The world seems to grow louder day by day, and our senses seem to be invaded at every turn. But, if we allow the distractions of a clamorous society to separate us from God's peace, we do ourselves a profound disservice. So if we're wise, we make time each day for quiet reflection. And when we do, we are rewarded.

Do you take time each day for an extended period of silence? And during those precious moments, do you sincerely open your heart to your Creator? If so, you will be blessed. If not, then the struggles and stresses of everyday living may rob you of the peace that should rightfully be yours because of your personal relationship with Christ. So take time each day to quietly commune with your Creator. When you do, those moments

of silence will enable you to participate more fully in the only
source of peace that endures: God's peace.

*I wait quietly before God,
for my salvation comes from him.*

Psalm 62:1 NLT

A TIP FOR GUARDING YOUR HEART

Want to talk to God? Then don't make Him shout. If you
really want to hear from God, go to a quiet place and listen.
If you keep listening long enough and carefully enough, He'll
start talking.

WORDS OF WISDOM

Deepest communion with God is beyond words, on the other side of silence.

Madeleine L'Engle

The world is full of noise. Might we not set ourselves to learn silence, stillness, solitude?

Elisabeth Elliot

Because Jesus Christ is our Great High Priest, not only can we approach God without a human "go-between," we can also hear and learn from God in some sacred moments without one.

Beth Moore

Growth takes place in quietness, in hidden ways, in silence and solitude. The process is not accessible to observation.

Eugene Peterson

There are times when to speak is to violate the moment—when silence represents the highest respect. The word for such times is reverence.

Max Lucado

GOD'S WORDS OF WISDOM

My soul, wait in silence for God only, for my hope is from Him.

Psalm 62:5 NASB

Be silent before Me.

Isaiah 41:1 Holman CSB

In quietness and trust is your strength.

Isaiah 30:15 NASB

What's this? Fools out shopping for wisdom! They wouldn't recognize it if they saw it! One Who Knows Much Says Little.

Proverbs 17:16 MSG

SUMMING IT UP

Spend a few moments each day in silence. You owe it to your Creator . . . and to yourself.

GUARD YOUR WORDS BY BEING KIND

Be kindly affectionate to one another with brotherly love,
in honor giving preference to one another; not lagging in diligence,
fervent in spirit, serving the Lord; rejoicing in hope,
patient in tribulation, continuing steadfastly in prayer.

Romans 12:10-12 NKJV

John Wesley's advice was straightforward: "Do all the good you can. By all the means you can. In all the ways you can. In all the places you can. At all the times you can. To all the people you can. As long as ever you can." One way to do all the good you can is to spread kindness wherever you go.

Sometimes, when we feel happy or generous, we find it easy to be kind. Other times, when we are discouraged or tired, we can scarcely summon the energy to utter a single kind word. But, God's commandment is clear: He intends that we make the conscious choice to treat others with kindness and respect, no matter our circumstances, no matter our emotions.

For Christians, kindness is not an option; it is a commandment. In the Gospel of Matthew, Jesus declares, "In everything, therefore, treat people the same way you want them to treat you, for this is the Law and the Prophets" (Matthew 7:12 NASB). Jesus did not say, "In some things, treat people as you wish to be treated." And, He did not say, "From time to time, treat others with kindness." Christ said that we should treat others as we wish to be treated "in everything." This, of course, is a difficult task, but as Christians, we are commanded to do our best.

Today, as you consider all the things that Christ has done in your life, honor Him by being a little kinder than necessary. Honor Him by slowing down long enough to offer encouragement to someone who needs it. Honor Him by picking up the phone and calling a distant friend . . . for no reason other than to say, "I'm thinking of you." Honor Christ with your good words and your good deeds. Jesus expects no less, and He deserves no less.

A gentle answer turns away wrath,
but a harsh word stirs up anger.

Proverbs 15:1 NIV

A TIP FOR GUARDING YOUR HEART

Kindness is more than good intentions. You've got to transform those good intentions into actions. Now.

WORDS OF WISDOM

Be so preoccupied with good will that you haven't room for ill will.

E. Stanley Jones

A little kindly advice is better than a great deal of scolding.

Fanny Crosby

If we have the true love of God in our hearts, we will show it in our lives. We will not have to go up and down the earth proclaiming it. We will show it in everything we say or do.

D. L. Moody

When you extend hospitality to others, you're not trying to impress people, you're trying to reflect God to them.

Max Lucado

It doesn't take monumental feats to make the world a better place. It can be as simple as letting someone go ahead of you in a grocery line.

Barbara Johnson

GOD'S WORDS OF WISDOM

I tell you the truth, whatever you did for one of the least of these brothers of mine, you did for me.

Matthew 25:40 NIV

And be ye kind one to another, tenderhearted, forgiving one another, even as God for Christ's sake hath forgiven you.

Ephesians 4:32 KJV

Refuse to get involved in inane discussions; they always end up in fights. God's servant must not be argumentative, but a gentle listener and a teacher who keeps cool, working firmly but patiently with those who refuse to obey.

2 Timothy 2:23-24 MSG

Show respect for all people. Love the brothers and sisters of God's family.

1 Peter 2:17 ICB

SUMMING IT UP

Kind words have echoes that last a lifetime and beyond.

GUARD YOUR WORDS BY REMAINING HUMBLE

Therefore humble yourselves under the mighty hand of God,
that He may exalt you in due time,
casting all your care upon Him, for He cares for you.

1 Peter 5:6-7 NKJV

If you desire to guard your heart, you must guard it against the sin of pride. Are you a humble believer who always gives credit where credit is due? If so, you are both wise and blessed.

Dietrich Bonhoeffer observed, "It is very easy to overestimate the importance of our own achievements in comparison with what we owe others." How true. Even those of us who consider ourselves "self-made" men and women are deeply indebted to more people than we can count. Our first and greatest indebtedness, of course, is to God and His only begotten Son. But we are also indebted to ancestors, parents, teachers, friends, spouses, family members, coworkers, fellow believers . . . and the list goes on.

With so many people who rightfully deserve to share the credit for our successes, how can we gloat? The answer, of course, is that we should not. But we inhabit a world in which far too many of our role models are remarkably haughty and surprisingly self-centered (hopefully, these are not your role models).

The Bible contains stern warnings against the sin of pride. One such warning is found in Proverbs 16:8: "Pride goes before destruction, and a haughty spirit before a fall" (NKJV). God's Word makes it clear: pride and destruction are traveling companions (but hopefully, they're not your traveling companions).

Jonathan Edwards observed, "Nothing sets a person so much out of the devil's reach as humility." So, if you're celebrating a worthwhile accomplishment, don't invite the devil to celebrate with you. Instead of puffing out your chest and saying, "Look at me!", give credit where credit is due, starting with God. And rest assured: There is no such thing as a self-made man. All of us are made by God . . . and He deserves the glory, not us.

A TIP FOR GUARDING YOUR HEART

Do you value humility above status? If so, God will smile upon your endeavors. But if you value status above humility, you're inviting God's displeasure. In short, humility pleases God; pride does not.

WORDS OF WISDOM

If you know who you are in Christ, your personal ego is not an issue.

Beth Moore

Jesus had a humble heart. If He abides in us, pride will never dominate our lives.

Billy Graham

Humility is the fairest and rarest flower that blooms.

Charles Swindoll

That's what I love about serving God. In His eyes, there are no little people . . . because there are no big people. We are all on the same playing field. We all start at square one. No one has it better than the other, or possesses unfair advantage.

Joni Eareckson Tada

All kindness and good deeds, we must keep silent. The result will be an inner reservoir of personality power.

Catherine Marshall

GOD'S WORDS OF WISDOM

Finally, all of you should be of one mind, full of sympathy toward each other, loving one another with tender hearts and humble minds.

1 Peter 3:8 NLT

Therefore humble yourselves under the mighty hand of God, that He may exalt you at the proper time, casting all your anxiety on Him, because He cares for you.

1 Peter 5:6-7 NASB

God has chosen you and made you his holy people. He loves you. So always do these things: Show mercy to others, be kind, humble, gentle, and patient.

Colossians 3:12 NCV

Do nothing out of rivalry or conceit, but in humility consider others as more important than yourselves.

Philippians 2:3 Holman CSB

SUMMING IT UP

You must remain humble or face the consequences. Pride does go before the fall, but humility often prevents the fall.

GUARD YOUR WORDS AGAINST PESSIMISM

The Lord is my light and my salvation; whom shall I fear?
The Lord is the strength of my life; of whom shall I be afraid?

Psalm 27:1 KJV

C hristians have every reason to be optimistic about life.
As Kay Arthur observed, "Joy is available to all who
seek His riches. The key to joy is found in the person of
Jesus Christ and in His will."

But, sometimes, rejoicing is the last thing on our minds.
Sometimes, we fall prey to worry, frustration, anxiety, or sheer
exhaustion . . . and our hearts become heavy. What's needed
is plenty of rest, a large dose of perspective, and God's healing
touch, but not necessarily in that order.

Hannah Whitall Smith noted, "The things we think are the
things that feed our souls. If we think on pure and lovely things,
we shall grow pure and lovely like them; and the converse
is equally true." These words remind us that even when the
challenges of the day seem daunting, God remains steadfast.
And, so must we.

Jesus offers us abundance and joy, but He doesn't force
abundance and joy upon us; we must claim these gifts for

ourselves. Today, why not claim the joy that is rightfully yours in Christ? Why not take time to celebrate God's glorious creation? When you do so, you will think optimistically about yourself and your world . . . and you can then share your optimism with others. You'll be better for it, and so will they.

So, the next time you find yourself dwelling upon the negative aspects of your life, refocus your attention on things positive. The next time you find yourself falling prey to the blight of pessimism, stop yourself and turn your thoughts around. The next time you're tempted to waste valuable time gossiping or complaining, resist those temptations with all your might. And remember: You'll never complain your way to the top . . . so don't waste your breath.

Make me hear joy and gladness.

Psalm 51:8 NKJV

A TIP FOR GUARDING YOUR HEART

Learn to look for opportunities, not obstructions; and while you're at it, look for possibilities, not problems.

WORDS OF WISDOM

There is wisdom in the habit of looking at the bright side of life.

Father Flanagan

Gratitude unlocks the fullness of life. It turns what we have into enough, and more. It turns denial into acceptance, chaos to order, confusion to clarity. It can turn a meal into a feast, a house into a home, a stranger into a friend. Gratitude makes sense of our past, brings peace for today, and creates a vision for tomorrow.

Melody Beattie

If you can't tell whether your glass is half-empty or half-full, you don't need another glass; what you need is better eyesight . . . and a more thankful heart.

Marie T. Freeman

The Christian lifestyle is not one of legalistic do's and don'ts, but one that is positive, attractive, and joyful.

Vonette Bright

The people whom I have seen succeed best in life have always been cheerful and hopeful people who went about their business with a smile on their faces.

Charles Kingsley

GOD'S WORDS OF WISDOM

But if we look forward to something we don't have yet, we must wait patiently and confidently.

Romans 8:25 NLT

My cup runs over. Surely goodness and mercy shall follow me all the days of my life; and I will dwell in the house of the Lord forever.

Psalm 23:5-6 NKJV

I can do everything through him that gives me strength.

Philippians 4:13 NIV

For God has not given us a spirit of fear, but of power and of love and of a sound mind.

2 Timothy 1:7 NLT

SUMMING IT UP

Optimism pays. Pessimism does not. Guard your thoughts and your words accordingly.

GUARD YOUR WORDS AGAINST THE TEMPTATION TO JUDGE

Do not judge, and you will not be judged. Do not condemn,
and you will not be condemned. Forgive, and you will be forgiven.

Luke 6:37 Holman CSB

Even the most devoted Christians may fall prey to a powerful yet subtle temptation: the temptation to judge others. But as believers, we are commanded to refrain from such behavior. The warning of Matthew 7:1 is clear: "Judge not, that ye be not judged" (KJV).

Are you one of those people who finds it easy to judge others? If so, it's time to make radical changes in the way you view the world and the people who inhabit it.

When considering the shortcomings of others, you must remember this: in matters of judgment, God does not need (or want) your help. Why? Because God is perfectly capable of judging the human heart . . . while you are not. This message is made clear by the teachings of Jesus.

As Jesus came upon a young woman who had been condemned by the Pharisees, He spoke not only to the crowd that was gathered there, but also to all generations, when He warned, "He that is without sin among you, let him first cast a stone at her" (John 8:7 KJV). Christ's message is clear: because we are all sinners, we are commanded to refrain from judging others. Yet the irony is this: it is precisely because we are sinners that we are so quick to judge.

All of us have all fallen short of God's laws, and none of us, therefore, are qualified to "cast the first stone." Thankfully, God has forgiven us, and we, too, must forgive others. Let us refrain, then, from judging our family members, our friends, and our loved ones. Instead, let us forgive them and love them in the same way that God has forgiven us.

A Tip for Guarding Your Heart

Remember: the ability to judge others requires a divine insight that you simply don't have.

WORDS OF WISDOM

God is the only judge. You are just his emissary of peace.

St. Thérèse of Lisieux

An individual Christian may see fit to give up all sorts of things for special reasons—marriage, or meat, or beer, or cinema; but the moment he starts saying these things are bad in themselves, or looking down his nose at other people who do use them, he has taken the wrong turn.

C. S. Lewis

Judging draws the judgment of others.

Catherine Marshall

No creed or school of thought can monopolize the Spirit of God.

Oswald Chambers

Turn your attention upon yourself and beware of judging the deeds of other men, for in judging others a man labors vainly, often makes mistakes, and easily sins; whereas, in judging and taking stock of himself he does something that is always profitable.

Thomas à Kempis

GOD'S WORDS OF WISDOM

The LORD does not look at the things man looks at. Man looks at the outward appearance, but the LORD looks at the heart.

1 Samuel 16:7 NIV

You, therefore, have no excuse, you who pass judgment on someone else, for at whatever point you judge the other, you are condemning yourself.

Romans 2:1 NIV

Speak and act as those who will be judged by the law of freedom. For judgment is without mercy to the one who hasn't shown mercy. Mercy triumphs over judgment.

James 2:12-13 Holman CSB

Therefore judge nothing before the time, until the Lord comes, who will both bring to light the hidden things of darkness and reveal the counsels of the hearts. Then each one's praise will come from God.

1 Corinthians 4:5 NKJV

SUMMING IT UP

To the extent you judge others, so, too, will you be judged. So you must, to the best of your ability, refrain from judgmental thoughts and words.

Guard Your Words Against Profanity

Avoid all perverse talk; stay far from corrupt speech.

Proverbs 4:24 NLT

Modern society seems to have fallen in love with profanity. You hear offensive language everywhere: on the radio, in the movie theater, on television (especially cable TV!), and in most public places. It seems that inappropriate language has infiltrated our culture at almost every level. And that's unfortunate.

Just because society embraces profanity doesn't mean that you should embrace it, too. In fact, the opposite should be true: the more vulgar the world becomes, the more determined you should be to avoid using profanity. Why? Because that's what God wants you to do.

Throughout the Bible, God gives many warnings about the use of inappropriate language. And if you're wise, you'll take those warnings to heart even if lots of people don't.

Oswald Chambers said, "The great test of a man's character is his tongue." Let these words serve to remind you that you should only use words that project who you are . . . a person of integrity and, more importantly, a Christian. So the next time you hear someone say something you wouldn't repeat in church, make sure that you don't join in. Profane words are against God's rules, and they should be against your rules, too.

Let the words of my mouth,
and the meditations of my heart,
be acceptable in thy sight, O Lord,
my strength and my redeemer.

Psalm 19:14 KJV

A TIP FOR GUARDING YOUR HEART

You live in a society that, for the most part, condones profanity—but you must not.

WORDS OF WISDOM

Fill the heart with the love of Christ so that only truth and purity can come out of the mouth.

Warren Wiersbe

I still believe we ought to talk about Jesus. The old country doctor of my boyhood days always began his examination by saying, "Let me see your tongue." That's a good way to check a Christian: the tongue test. Let's hear what he is talking about.

Vance Havner

When you talk, choose the very same words that you would use if Jesus were looking over your shoulder. Because He is.

Marie T. Freeman

It is time that the followers of Jesus revise their language and learn to speak respectfully of non-Christian peoples.

Lottie Moon

Attitude and the spirit in which we communicate are as important as the words we say.

Charles Stanley

GOD'S WORDS OF WISDOM

But I say unto you, That every idle word that men shall speak, they shall give account thereof in the day of judgment. For by thy words thou shalt be justified, and by thy words thou shalt be condemned.

Matthew 12:36-37 KJV

Reckless words pierce like a sword, but the tongue of the wise brings healing.

Proverbs 12:18 NIV

To everything there is a season . . . a time to keep silence, and a time to speak.

Ecclesiastes 3:1, 7 KJV

For out of the overflow of the heart the mouth speaks.

Matthew 12:34 NIV

SUMMING IT UP

Profanity has absolutely no place in your vocabulary. Period.

GUARD YOUR WORDS AGAINST BITTERNESS

*Get rid of all bitterness, rage, anger, harsh words,
and slander, as well as all types of malicious behavior.
Instead, be kind to each other, tenderhearted, forgiving one another,
just as God through Christ has forgiven you.*

Ephesians 4:31-32 NLT

D o you value the role that forgiveness can play in your
life? Hopefully so. But even if you're a dedicated
believer, you may have a difficult time forgiving those
who have hurt you. If you're one of those folks who, despite your
best intentions, has a difficult time forgiving and forgetting, you
are not alone.

Life would be much simpler if we humans could forgive
people "once and for all" and be done with it. But forgiveness
is seldom that easy. For most people, the decision to forgive is
straightforward, but the process of forgiving is more difficult.
Forgiveness is a journey that requires effort, time, perseverance,
and prayer.

Sometimes, it's not "the other person" whom you need to
forgive; it's yourself. If you've made mistakes (And who among

us hasn't?), perhaps you're continuing to bear a grudge against the person in the mirror. If so, here's a three-step process for resolving those feelings:

1. Stop the harmful behavior that is the source of your self-directed anger.
2. Seek forgiveness from God (and from any people whom you may have hurt).
3. Ask God to cleanse your heart of all bitterness and regret . . . and keep asking Him until your feelings of anger and regret are gone.

If there exists even one person, alive or dead, whom you have not forgiven (and that includes yourself), follow God's commandment: forgive that person today. And remember that bitterness, anger, and regret are not part of God's plan for your life. Forgiveness is.

Perhaps you need a refresher course in the art of forgiveness. If so, it's time to open your Bible and your heart. When you do, you'll discover that God can heal your broken spirit. Don't expect forgiveness to be easy or quick, but rest assured that with God as your partner, you can forgive . . . and you will.

A TIP FOR GUARDING YOUR HEART

Today, make a list of the people you still need to forgive. Then make up your mind to forgive at least one person on that list. Finally, ask God to cleanse your heart of bitterness, animosity, and regret. If you ask Him sincerely and often, He will respond.

WORDS OF WISDOM

Revenge is the raging fire that consumes the arsonist.

Max Lucado

The more you practice the art of forgiving, the quicker you'll master the art of living.

Marie T. Freeman

Our forgiveness toward others should flow from a realization and appreciation of God's forgiveness toward us.

Franklin Graham

To hold on to hate and resentments is to throw a monkey wrench into the machinery of life.

E. Stanley Jones

I firmly believe a great many prayers are not answered because we are not willing to forgive someone.

D. L. Moody

GOD'S WORDS OF WISDOM

*Be even-tempered, content with second place, quick to forgive an
offense. Forgive as quickly and completely as the Master forgave you.
And regardless of what else you put on, wear love. It's your basic,
all-purpose garment. Never be without it.*

Colossians 3:13-14 MSG

Hatred stirs up trouble, but love forgives all wrongs.

Proverbs 10:12 NCV

*Our Father is kind; you be kind. "Don't pick on people, jump on their
failures, criticize their faults—unless, of course, you want the same
treatment. Don't condemn those who are down; that hardness can
boomerang. Be easy on people; you'll find life a lot easier."*

Luke 6:36-37 MSG

*Whenever you stand praying, forgive, if you have anything against
anyone, so that your Father in heaven will also forgive you your
transgressions.*

Mark 11:25 NASB

SUMMING IT UP

Forgiveness is its own reward. Bitterness is its own
punishment. Guard your words and your thoughts
accordingly.

GUARD YOUR WORDS WITH INTEGRITY

The integrity of the upright will guide them.

Proverbs 11:3 NKJV

Catherine Marshall correctly observed, "The single most important element in any human relationship is honesty—with oneself, with God, and with others." Godly men and women agree. As believers in Christ, we must seek to live each day with discipline, honesty, and faith. When we do, at least two things happen: integrity becomes a habit, and God blesses us because of our obedience to Him. Living a life of integrity isn't always the easiest way, but it is always the right way . . . and God clearly intends that it should be our way, too.

Character isn't built overnight; it is built slowly over a lifetime. It is the sum of every right decision and every honest word. It is forged on the anvil of honorable work and polished by the twin virtues of honesty and fairness. Character is a precious thing—difficult to build and wonderful to behold.

Oswald Chambers, the author of the Christian classic text, *My Utmost For His Highest*, advised, "Never support an experience which does not have God as its source, and faith in God as its result." These words serve as a powerful reminder that as Christians we are called to walk with God and to obey His commandments. But, we live in a world that presents us with countless temptations to wander far from God's path. These temptations have the potential to destroy us, in part, because they cause us to be dishonest with ourselves and with others.

Dishonesty is a habit. Once we start bending the truth, we're likely to keep bending it. A far better strategy, of course, is to acquire the habit of being completely forthright with God, with other people, and with ourselves.

Honesty is also a habit, a habit that pays powerful dividends for those who place character above convenience. So, the next time you're tempted to bend the truth—or to break it—ask yourself this simple question: "What does God want me to do?" Then listen carefully to your conscience. When you do, your actions will be honorable, and your character will take care of itself.

A TIP FOR GUARDING YOUR HEART

Character matters: Your ability to witness for Christ depends more upon your actions than your words.

WORDS OF WISDOM

Each one of us is God's special work of art. Through us, He teaches and inspires, delights and encourages, informs and uplifts all those who view our lives. God, the master artist, is most concerned about expressing Himself—His thoughts and His intentions—through what He paints in our characters.

Joni Eareckson Tada

A solid trust is based on a consistent character.

John Maxwell

It is the thoughts and intents of the heart that shape a person's life.

John Eldredge

Character cannot be developed in ease and quiet. Only through experience of trial and suffering can the soul be strengthened, vision cleared, ambition inspired, and success achieved.

Helen Keller

What we are is more significant, in the long run, than what we do. It is impossible for a man to give what he does not have.

Elton Trueblood

GOD'S WORDS OF WISDOM

Do not be misled: "Bad company corrupts good character."

1 Corinthians 15:33 NIV

Applying all diligence, in your faith supply moral excellence.

2 Peter 1:5 NASB

The righteousness of the blameless clears his path, but the wicked person will fall because of his wickedness.

Proverbs 11:5 Holman CSB

A good name is more desirable than great riches; to be esteemed is better than silver or gold.

Proverbs 22:1 NIV

We also have joy with our troubles, because we know that these troubles produce patience. And patience produces character, and character produces hope.

Romans 5:3-4 NCV

SUMMING IT UP

When your words are honest and your intentions are pure, you have nothing to fear. Thus, you should guard your integrity even more carefully than you guard your wallet.

GUARD YOUR WORDS AGAINST ANGER

Refrain from anger and turn from wrath;
do not fret—it leads only to evil.

Psalm 37:8 NIV

Because we are imperfect human beings living among other imperfect human beings, we encounter countless frustrations, some great and some small. On occasion, we confront imminent evil, and when we do, we should respond vigorously and without reservation. But more often than not, our challenges are much more mundane. We are confronted, not by impending evil, but by the inevitable distractions and disappointments of life here on earth: jammed traffic, spilled coffee, and similar inconveniences. Our challenge is this: to display anger when it is appropriate and to rein in our tempers when it is not.

How can we learn to maintain better control over our tempers? By using focus, forgiveness, and faith. We must learn to focus our thoughts, not on the inevitable disappointments of life, but instead upon the innumerable blessings that God has given us. In other words, we must learn to look carefully at the donut, not the hole. And we must learn to forgive. When we forgive others thoroughly and often, we avoid the anger-provoking traps of bitterness and regret. Faith, too, is an antidote to anger. When we allow our faith in God to become the cornerstone and the touchstone of our lives, we cultivate an unwavering trust in the righteous of His plans. When we do so, we begin to see God's hand as it works in every aspect of our lives—in good times and in hard times—as He uses every circumstance to fulfill His plan for us.

Sometimes we are victims of secondhand anger. We may become angry because someone else is angry. Why does this occur? Because anger is a highly contagious emotion. When we spend time with angry people, we, too, tend to become angry. Once again, God's Word offers a solution that doubles as a warning: "Make no friendship with an angry man" (Proverbs 22:24 NKJV).

The next time you are tempted to lose your temper over the minor inconveniences of life, don't. Turn away from angry people and angry thoughts. Turn instead to God. Choose forgiveness instead of hatred; choose acceptance, not regret; let the assurance of God's eternal promises overcome the inevitability of life's fleeting disappointments. When you do, you'll give yourself a priceless gift: the gift of peace. And God will smile.

A TIP FOR GUARDING YOUR HEART

You can control your temper . . . if you try: If you think your temper is some sort of raging, uncontrollable beast, you're mistaken. You can control your anger, and that's precisely what you should learn to do. The next time you're tempted to explode in anger, slow down, catch your breath, and walk away if you must. It's better to walk away—and keep walking—than it is to blurt out angry words that can't be un-blurted.

WORDS OF WISDOM

Life is too short to spend it being angry, bored, or dull.

Barbara Johnson

When you strike out in anger, you may miss the other person, but you will always hit yourself.

Jim Gallery

Why lose your temper if, by doing so, you offend God, annoy other people, give yourself a bad time . . . and, in the end, have to find it again?

Josemaria Escriva

When something robs you of your peace of mind, ask yourself if it is worth the energy you are expending on it. If not, then put it out of your mind in an act of discipline. Every time the thought of "it" returns, refuse it.

Kay Arthur

Is there somebody who's always getting your goat? Talk to the Shepherd.

Anonymous

GOD'S WORDS OF WISDOM

And the servant of the Lord must not strive; but be gentle unto all men, apt to teach, patient; in meekness instructing those that oppose themselves . . . .

2 Timothy 2:24-25 KJV

My dear brothers and sisters, always be willing to listen and slow to speak. Do not become angry easily, because anger will not help you live the right kind of life God wants.

James 1:19-20 NCV

A patient man has great understanding, but a quick-tempered man displays folly.

Proverbs 14:29 NIV

But I tell you that anyone who is angry with his brother is subject to judgment.

Matthew 5:22 NIV

SUMMING IT UP

Angry words are dangerous to your emotional and spiritual health, not to mention your relationships. So treat anger as an uninvited guest, and usher it away as quickly—and as quietly—as possible.

GUARD YOUR WORDS BY ENCOURAGING OTHERS

When you talk, do not say harmful things, but say what people need—words that will help others become stronger. Then what you say will do good to those who listen to you.

Ephesians 4:29 NCV

In his letter to the Ephesians, Paul writes, "Do not let any unwholesome talk come out of your mouths, but only what is helpful for building others up according to their needs, that it may benefit those who listen" (4:29 NIV). This passage reminds us that, as Christians, we are instructed to choose our words carefully in order that we might build others up through wholesome, honest encouragement.

One of the best ways to build others up is by celebrating their accomplishments. As the old saying goes, "When someone does something good, applaud—you'll make two people happy." But sometimes, we don't feel much like applauding. At times, we're simply too tired or too discouraged to be of much help to others. Yet even on our darkest days, even on those days when we find it difficult to muster even a single kind word, we should strive to follow the physicians' creed: Do no harm.

It's worth noting that the art of encouragement is not a skill that can be acquired overnight; it is a skill that is learned over time and improved with constant use. Nonetheless, we may encounter situations that leave us puzzled—we simply do not know what to say or do. How, we ask, can we be most encouraging? The answer is found, in part, by reminding ourselves what genuine encouragement is and what it is not.

The dictionary defines encouragement as, "the act of inspiring courage and confidence." As Christians, we must first seek to inspire others' confidence in God and in His Son Jesus Christ. We are comforted by the knowledge that God's gifts are too numerous to count and that His love extends to all generations—including our own. While our greatest encouragement comes from the assurance of God's power and His promises, we can also find encouragement when we are reminded of our own abilities and strengths. Genuine encouragement is not idle flattery; it is simply a firm reminder of the talents that God has given each of us and of our need to use those talents wisely.

Genuine encouragement should never be confused with pity. God intends for His children to lead lives of abundance, joy, celebration and praise—not lives of self-pity or regret. So we must guard ourselves against hosting (or joining) the "pity parties" that so often accompany difficult times. Instead, we must encourage each other to have faith—first in God and his only begotten Son—and then in our own abilities to use the talents God has given us for the furtherance of His kingdom and for the betterment of our own lives.

WORDS OF WISDOM

Encouragement starts at home, but it should never end there.

Marie T. Freeman

If I am asked how we are to get rid of discouragements, I can only say, as I have had to say of so many other wrong spiritual habits, we must give them up. It is never worth while to argue against discouragement. There is only one argument that can meet it, and that is the argument of God.

Hannah Whitall Smith

A single word, if spoken in a friendly spirit, may be sufficient to turn one from dangerous error.

Fanny Crosby

It is helpful to remember the distinction between appreciation and affirmation. We appreciate what a person does, but we affirm who a person is.

Charles Swindoll

A TIP FOR GUARDING YOUR HEART

Encouragement is contagious. You can't lift other people up without lifting yourself up, too.

GOD'S WORDS OF WISDOM

Let the word of Christ dwell in you richly in all wisdom; teaching and admonishing one another in psalms and hymns and spiritual songs, singing with grace in your hearts to the Lord.

Colossians 3:16 KJV

Let us consider how to stimulate one another to love and good deeds.

Hebrews 10:24 NASB

We urge you, brethren, admonish the unruly, encourage the fainthearted, help the weak, be patient with everyone.

1 Thessalonians 5:14 NASB

Anxiety in a man's heart weighs it down, but a good word cheers it up.

Proverbs 12:25 Holman CSB

SUMMING IT UP

Your friends and family members need encouraging words . . . from you.

GUARD YOUR WORDS WITH CONSTANT PRAISE FOR THE CREATOR

Praise the Lord! Oh, give thanks to the Lord, for He is good!
For His mercy endures forever.

Psalm 106:1 NKJV

A wonderful way to guard your heart is by praising God. And when is the best time to praise God? In church? Before dinner is served? When we tuck little children into bed? None of the above. The best time to praise God is all day, every day, to the greatest extent we can, with thanksgiving in our hearts, and with a song on our lips.

Too many of us, even well-intentioned believers, tend to "compartmentalize" our waking hours into a few familiar categories: work, rest, play, family time, and worship. To do so is a mistake. Worship and praise should be woven into the fabric of everything we do; it should never be relegated to a weekly three-hour visit to church on Sunday morning.

The words by Fanny Crosby are familiar: "This is my story, this is my song, praising my Savior, all the day long." As believers who have been saved by the sacrifice of a risen Christ, we must do exactly as the song instructs: We must praise our Savior time and time again throughout the day. Worship and praise should be a part of everything we do. Otherwise, we quickly lose perspective as we fall prey to the demands of everyday life.

Theologian Wayne Oates once admitted, "Many of my prayers are made with my eyes open. You see, it seems I'm always praying about something, and it's not always convenient—or safe—to close my eyes." Dr. Oates understood that God always hears our prayers and that the relative position of our eyelids is of no concern to Him.

Do you sincerely desire to be a worthy servant of the One who has given you eternal love and eternal life? Then praise Him for who He is and for what He has done for you. And don't just praise Him on Sunday morning. Praise Him all day long, every day, for as long as you live . . . and then for all eternity.

A TIP FOR GUARDING YOUR HEART

If you're a thoughtful believer, you'll make it a habit to praise God many times each day, beginning with your morning devotional.

WORDS OF WISDOM

Nothing we do is more powerful or more life-changing than praising God.

Stormie Omartian

Our God is the sovereign Creator of the universe! He loves us as His own children and has provided every good thing we have; He is worthy of our praise every moment.

Shirley Dobson

Holy, holy, holy! Lord God Almighty! All Thy works shall praise Thy name in earth, and sky, and sea.

Reginald Heber

Praise is the highest occupation of any being.

Max Lucado

The best moment to praise God is always the present one.

Marie T. Freeman

GOD'S WORDS OF WISDOM

Is anyone happy? Let him sing songs of praise.

James 5:13 NIV

Through Him then, let us continually offer up a sacrifice of praise to God, that is, the fruit of lips that give thanks to His name.

Hebrews 13:15 NASB

The LORD is my strength and song, and He has become my salvation; He is my God, and I will praise Him.

Exodus 15:2 NIV

And suddenly there was with the angel a multitude of the heavenly host praising God and saying: "Glory to God in the highest, And on earth peace, goodwill toward men!"

Luke 2:13-14 NKJV

At the name of Jesus every knee should bow, of those in heaven, and of those on earth, and of those under the earth, and that every tongue should confess that Jesus Christ is Lord, to the glory of God the Father.

Philippians 2:10-11 NKJV

SUMMING IT UP

The appropriate moment to praise God is always this one.

PART 2

GUARD
YOUR EYES

GUARD YOUR EYES AGAINST THE WORLD'S MANY TEMPTATIONS

Put on the whole armor of God,
that you may be able to stand against the wiles of the devil.

Ephesians 6:11 NKJV

Because our world is filled with temptations, we confront them at every turn. Some of these temptations are small—eating a second piece of chocolate cake, for example. Too much cake may cause us to defile, at least in a modest way, the bodily temple that God has entrusted to our care. But two pieces of cake will not bring us to our knees. Other temptations, however, are not so harmless.

The devil, it seems, is working overtime these days, and causing heartache in more places and in more ways than ever before. We, as Christians, must remain vigilant. Not only must we resist Satan when he confronts us, but we must also avoid those places where Satan can most easily tempt us. And, if we are to avoid the unending temptations of this world, we must arm ourselves with the Word of God.

In a letter to believers, Peter offered a stern warning: "Be sober, be vigilant; because your adversary the devil walks about like a roaring lion, seeking whom he may devour." (1 Peter 5:8 NKJV). What was true in New Testament times is equally true in our own. Satan tempts his prey and then devours them. And in these dangerous times, the tools that Satan uses to destroy his prey are more numerous than ever before.

As Christians, we must beware. And, if we seek righteousness in our own lives, we must earnestly wrap ourselves in the protection of God's Holy Word. After fasting forty days and nights in the desert, Jesus Himself was tempted by Satan. Christ used scripture to rebuke the devil (Matthew 4:1-11). We must do likewise. The Holy Bible provides us with a perfect blueprint for righteous living. If we consult that blueprint each day and follow its instructions carefully, we build our lives according to God's plan. And when we do, we are secure.

A Tip for Guarding Your Heart

If life's inevitable temptations seem to be getting the best of you, try praying more often, even if many of those prayers are simple, brief, "open-eyed" requests to your Father in heaven.

WORDS OF WISDOM

Do not fight the temptation in detail. Turn from it. Look ONLY at your Lord. Sing. Read. Work.

Amy Carmichael

Because Christ has faced our every temptation without sin, we never face a temptation that has no door of escape.

Beth Moore

Man without God is always torn between two urges. His nature prompts him to do wrong, and his conscience urges him to do right. Christ can rid you of that inner conflict.

Billy Graham

Since you are tempted without ceasing, pray without ceasing.

C. H. Spurgeon

Lord, what joy to know that Your powers are so much greater than those of the enemy.

Corrie ten Boom

GOD'S WORDS OF WISDOM

But remember that the temptations that come into your life are no different from what others experience. And God is faithful. He will keep the temptation from becoming so strong that you can't stand up against it. When you are tempted, he will show you a way out so that you will not give in to it.

1 Corinthians 10:13 NLT

For we do not have a High Priest who cannot sympathize with our weaknesses, but was in all points tempted as we are, yet without sin. Let us therefore come boldly to the throne of grace, that we may obtain mercy and find grace to help in time of need.

Hebrews 4:15-16 NKJV

My child, if sinners try to lead you into sin, do not follow them.

Proverbs 1:10 NCV

So let God work his will in you. Yell a loud no to the Devil and watch him scamper. Say a quiet yes to God and he'll be there in no time. Quit dabbling in sin. Purify your inner life. Quit playing the field.

James 4:7-8 MSG

SUMMING IT UP

Because you live in a temptation-filled world, you must guard your eyes, your thoughts, and your heart—all day, every day.

GUARD YOUR EYES AGAINST MATERIALISM

Do not love the world or the things in the world.
If anyone loves the world, the love of the Father is not in him.

1 John 2:15 NKJV

In our modern society, we need money to live. But as
Christians, we must never make the acquisition of money
the central focus of our lives. Money is a tool, but it should
never overwhelm our sensibilities. The focus of life must be
squarely on things spiritual, not things material.

Whenever we place our love for material possessions above
our love for God—or when we yield to the countless other
temptations of everyday living—we find ourselves engaged in a
struggle between good and evil. Let us respond to this struggle by
freeing ourselves from that subtle yet powerful temptation: the
temptation to love the world more than we love God.

Ask yourself this simple question: "Do I own my possessions,
or do they own me?" If you don't like the answer you receive,
make an iron-clad promise to stop acquiring and start divesting.
As you simplify your life, you'll be amazed at the things you
can do without. You'll be pleasantly surprised at the sense of
satisfaction that accompanies your new-found moderation. And
you'll understand first-hand that when it comes to material

possessions, less truly is more.

How important are our material possessions? Not as important as we might think. In the lives of committed Christians, material possessions should play a rather small role. Of course, we all need the basic necessities of life, but once we meet those needs for ourselves and for our families, the piling up of possessions creates more problems than it solves. Our real riches, of course, are not of this world. We are never really rich until we are rich in spirit.

So, if you find yourself wrapped up in the concerns of the material world, it's time to reorder your priorities by turning your thoughts and your prayers to more important matters. And, it's time to begin storing up riches that will endure throughout eternity: the spiritual kind.

A TIP FOR GUARDING YOUR HEART

Do you find yourself wrapped up in the material world? If so, it's time to reorder your priorities and reassess your values. Today, think long and hard about the priorities and values that guide your decision-making. And then, when you finally put all that material stuff in perspective, begin storing up riches that will endure throughout eternity—the spiritual kind.

WORDS OF WISDOM

Greed is enslaving. The more you have, the more you want—
until eventually avarice consumes you.

Kay Arthur

As faithful stewards of what we have, ought we not to give
earnest thought to our staggering surplus?

Elisabeth Elliot

The cross is laid on every Christian. It begins with the call to
abandon the attachments of this world.

Dietrich Bonhoeffer

There is absolutely no evidence that complexity and materialism
lead to happiness. On the contrary, there is plenty of evidence
that simplicity and spirituality lead to joy, a blessedness that is
better than happiness.

Dennis Swanberg

If you want to be truly happy, you won't find it on an endless
quest for more stuff. You'll find it in receiving God's generosity
and in the passing that generosity along.

Bill Hybels

GOD'S WORDS OF WISDOM

And He told them, "Watch out and be on guard against all greed, because one's life is not in the abundance of his possessions.

Luke 12:15 Holman CSB

He who trusts in his riches will fall, but the righteous will flourish . . . .

Proverbs 11:28 NKJV

No one can serve two masters. The person will hate one master and love the other, or will follow one master and refuse to follow the other. You cannot serve both God and worldly riches.

Matthew 6:24 NCV

For the mind-set of the flesh is death, but the mind-set of the Spirit is life and peace.

Romans 8:6 Holman CSB

Since we entered the world penniless and will leave it penniless, if we have bread on the table and shoes on our feet, that's enough.

1 Timothy 6:7-8 MSG

SUMMING IT UP

Material possessions may seem appealing at first, but they pale in comparison to the spiritual gifts that God gives to those who put Him first. Count yourself among that number.

GUARD YOUR EYES AGAINST THE MEDIA MADNESS

Do not love the world or the things that belong to the world.
If anyone loves the world, love for the Father is not in him.
Because everything that belongs to the world—the lust of the flesh,
the lust of the eyes, and the pride in one's lifestyle—
is not from the Father, but is from the world.

1 John 2:15-16 Holman CSB

I f you and your loved ones have acquired the bad habit of watching whatever happens to pop up on you family's TV screen, it's time to rethink the way you control your clicker. Most television networks (as well as the other forms of popular media) can be dangerous to your emotional and spiritual health.

The media is working around the clock in an attempt to rearrange your family's priorities in ways that are definitely not in your best interests. The media is trying to teach your family that physical appearance is all-important, that material possessions should be acquired at any cost, and that the world operates independently of God's laws. But guess what? Those messages are lies.

In the pursuit of profits, the media glamorizes violence, exploits suffering, and sensationalizes sex, all in the name of "ratings" (translated: "money").

So here's a question for you and your family: Will you control what appears on your TV screen, or will you be controlled by it? If you're willing to take complete control over the images that appear inside the four walls of your home, you'll be doing yourselves a king-sized favor. So forget the media hype, and pay attention to God. Stand up for Him and be counted, not just in church where it's relatively easy to be a Christian, but also when you're deciding what to watch. You owe it to your Creator . . . and you owe it to yourselves.

Do not have other gods besides Me.

Exodus 20:3 Holman CSB

A TIP FOR GUARDING YOUR HEART

Make God the cornerstone of your home, and watch programming that reinforces the principles set forth in God's Word.

WORDS OF WISDOM

The true Christian, though he is in revolt against the world's efforts to brainwash him, is no mere rebel for rebellion's sake. He dissents from the world because he knows that it cannot make good on its promises.

A. W. Tozer

Every day, I find countless opportunities to decide whether I will obey God and demonstrate my love for Him or try to please myself or the world system. God is waiting for my choices.

Bill Bright

Too many Christians have geared their program to please, to entertain, and to gain favor from this world. We are concerned with how much, instead of how little, like this age we can become.

Billy Graham

The more we stuff ourselves with material pleasures, the less we seem to appreciate life.

Barbara Johnson

GOD'S WORDS OF WISDOM

Let no one deceive himself. If anyone among you seems to be wise in this age, let him become a fool that he may become wise. For the wisdom of this world is foolishness with God. For it is written, "He catches the wise in their own craftiness."

1 Corinthians 3:18–19 NKJV

For whatever is born of God overcomes the world. And this is the victory that has overcome the world—our faith.

1 John 5:4 NKJV

Religion that God our Father accepts as pure and faultless is this: to look after orphans and widows in their distress and to keep oneself from being polluted by the world.

James 1:27 NIV

If you lived on the world's terms, the world would love you as one of its own. But since I picked you to live on God's terms and no longer on the world's terms, the world is going to hate you.

John 15:19 MSG

SUMMING IT UP

The popular media has a way of attacking your senses and your heart. Approach the media with care.

GUARD YOUR EYES BY CLOSING THEM AT A SENSIBLE HOUR

Come to me, all you who are weary and burdened,
and I will give you rest. Take my yoke upon you and learn from me,
for I am gentle and humble in heart, and you will find rest
for your souls. For my yoke is easy and my burden is light.

Matthew 11:28-30 NIV

Even the most energetic Christians can, from time to time, find themselves running on empty. The demands of daily life can drain us of our strength and rob us of the joy that is rightfully ours in Christ. When we find ourselves tired, discouraged, or worse, there is a source from which we can draw the power needed to recharge our spiritual batteries. That source is God.

God intends that His children lead joyous lives filled with abundance and peace. But sometimes, abundance and peace seem very far away. It is then that we must turn to God for renewal, and when we do, He will restore us.

Physical exhaustion is God's way of telling us to slow down. God expects us to work hard, of course, but He also intends for us to rest. When we fail to take the rest that we need, we do a disservice to ourselves and to our families.

We live in a world that tempts us to stay up late—very late. But too much late-night TV, combined with too little sleep, is a prescription for exhaustion.

Are your physical or spiritual batteries running low? Is your energy on the wane? Are your emotions frayed? If so, it's time to turn your thoughts and your prayers to God. And when you're finished, it's probably time to turn off the lights and go to bed!

*I will give you a new heart
and put a new spirit within you.*

Ezekiel 36:26 Holman CSB

A TIP FOR GUARDING YOUR HEART

It takes energy to do God's work; exhaustion is not God's way. Remember: a well-rested Christian can be a much more effective worker for God.

WORDS OF WISDOM

Jesus taught us by example to get out of the rat race and recharge our batteries.

Barbara Johnson

Notice what Jesus had to say concerning those who have wearied themselves by trying to do things in their own strength: "Come to me, all you who labor and are heavy laden, and I will give you rest."

Henry Blackaby and Claude King

Thou hast formed us for Thyself, and our hearts are restless till they find rest in Thee.

St. Augustine

Satan does some of his worst work on exhausted Christians when nerves are frayed and their minds are faint.

Vance Havner

If we stay with the Lord, enduring to the end of His great plan for us, we will enjoy the rest that results from living in the kingdom of God.

Serita Ann Jakes

GOD'S WORDS OF WISDOM

The One who was sitting on the throne said, "Look! I am making everything new!" Then he said, "Write this, because these words are true and can be trusted."

Revelation 21:5 NCV

When doubts filled my mind, your comfort gave me renewed hope and cheer.

Psalm 94:19 NLT

Create in me a pure heart, O God, and renew a steadfast spirit within me. Do not cast me from your presence or take your Holy Spirit from me. Restore to me the joy of your salvation and grant me a willing spirit, to sustain me.

Psalm 51:10-12 NIV

He makes me to lie down in green pastures; He leads me beside the still waters. He restores my soul; He leads me in the paths of righteousness For His name's sake.

Psalm 23:2–3 NKJV

SUMMING IT UP

Your body, which is a priceless gift from God, needs a sensible amount of sleep each night. Schedule your life accordingly.

GUARD YOUR EYES AGAINST ENVY

But if you harbor bitter envy and selfish ambition in your hearts,
do not boast about it or deny the truth. Such "wisdom" does not
come down from heaven but is earthly, unspiritual, of the devil.
For where you have envy and selfish ambition,
there you find disorder and every evil practice.

James 3:14-17 NIV

Because we are frail, imperfect human beings, we are sometimes envious of others. But God's Word warns us that envy is sin. Thus, we must guard ourselves against the natural tendency to feel resentment and jealousy when other people experience good fortune.

As believers, we have absolutely no reason to be envious of any people on earth. After all, as Christians we are already recipients of the greatest gift in all creation: God's grace. We have been promised the gift of eternal life through God's only begotten Son, and we must count that gift as our most precious possession.

St. Augustine, noted, "Whoever possesses God is happy." So here's a simple suggestion that is guaranteed to bring you happiness: fill your heart with God's love, God's promises, and

God's Son . . . and when you do so, leave no room for envy, hatred, bitterness, or regret.

As the recipient of God's grace, you have every reason to celebrate life. After all, God has promised you the opportunity to receive His abundance and His joy—in fact, you have the opportunity to receive those gifts right now. But if you allow envy to gnaw away at the fabric of your soul, you'll find that joy remains elusive. So do yourself an enormous favor: Rather than succumbing to the sin of envy, focus on the marvelous things that God has done for you—starting with Christ's sacrifice. Thank the Giver of all good gifts, and keep thanking Him for the wonders of His love and the miracles of His creation. When you do, you'll soon discover that the emotions of gratitude and envy are mutually exclusive.

So, if you want a simple, surefire formula for a happier, healthier life, here it is: Count your own blessings and let your neighbors counts theirs. It's the godly way to live.

A TIP FOR GUARDING YOUR HEART

You'll never be happy . . . if you spend more time counting your neighbor's blessings than you spend counting your own.

WORDS OF WISDOM

Too many Christians envy the sinners their pleasure and the saints their joy because they don't have either one.

Martin Luther

As a moth gnaws a garment, so does envy consume a man.

St. John Chrysostom

What God asks, does, or requires of others is not my business; it is His.

Kay Arthur

Contentment comes when we develop an attitude of gratitude for the important things we do have in our lives that we tend to take for granted if we have our eyes staring longingly at our neighbor's stuff.

Dave Ramsey

When you worry about what you don't have, you won't be able to enjoy what you do have.

Charles Swindoll

GOD'S WORDS OF WISDOM

Do not covet your neighbor's house . . . or anything that belongs to your neighbor.

Exodus 20:17 Holman CSB

Stop your anger! Turn from your rage! Do not envy others—it only leads to harm.

Psalm 37:8 NLT

We must not become conceited, provoking one another, envying one another.

Galatians 5:26 Holman CSB

If your sinful nature controls your mind, there is death. But if the Holy Spirit controls your mind, there is life and peace.

Romans 8:6 NLT

I have told you these things, so that in me you may have peace. In this world you will have trouble. But take heart! I have overcome the world.

John 16:33 NIV

SUMMING IT UP

Envy is a sin, a sin that robs you of contentment and peace. So you must refuse to let feelings of envy invade your thoughts or your heart.

Guard Your Eyes by Looking Straight Ahead

Look straight ahead, and fix your eyes on what lies before you.

Proverbs 4:25 NLT

Sometimes sin has a way of sneaking up on us. In the beginning, we don't intend to rebel against God—in fact, we don't think much about God at all. We think, instead, about the allure of sin, and we think (quite incorrectly) that sin is "harmless."

If we deny our sins, we allow those sins to flourish. And if we allow sinful behaviors to become habits, we invite certain hardships into our own lives and into the lives of our loved ones.

Sin tears down character. When we yield to the distractions and temptations of this troubled world, we suffer. But God has other intentions, and His plans for our lives do not include sin or denial.

As creatures of free will, we may disobey God whenever we choose, but when we do so, we put ourselves and our loved ones in peril. Why? Because disobedience invites disaster. We cannot sin against God without consequence. We cannot live outside

His will without injury. We cannot distance ourselves from God without hardening our hearts. We cannot yield to the ever-tempting distractions of our world and, at the same time, enjoy God's peace.

Sometimes, in a futile attempt to justify our behaviors, we make a distinction between "big" sins and "little" ones. To do so is a mistake of "big" proportions. Sins of all shapes and sizes have the power to do us great harm. And in a world where sin is big business, that's certainly a sobering thought.

If we say that we have no sin, we deceive ourselves, and the truth is not in us. If we confess our sins, He is faithful and just to forgive us our sins and to cleanse us from all unrighteousness.

1 John 1:8-9 NKJV

A Tip for Guarding Your Heart

Always avoid people and places that might tempt you to disobey God's commandments.

WORDS OF WISDOM

Let us never suppose that obedience is impossible or that holiness is meant only for a select few. Our Shepherd leads us in paths of righteousness—not for our name's sake but for His.

Elisabeth Elliot

There is nothing wrong with asking God's direction. But it is wrong to go our own way, then expect Him to bail us out.

Larry Burkett

Identify the sin. Confess it. Turn from it. Avoid it at all costs. Live with a clean, forgiven conscience. Don't dwell on what God has forgotten!

Max Lucado

Sin must be destroyed, not corrected.

Oswald Chambers

Sin will take you farther than you'll want to go; sin will leave you longer than you'll want to stay; sin will cost you far more than you'll want to pay.

Anonymous

GOD'S WORDS OF WISDOM

Whoever transgresses and does not abide in the doctrine of Christ does not have God. He who abides in the doctrine of Christ has both the Father and the Son.

2 John 1:9 NKJV

Let us lay aside every weight, and the sin which so easily ensnares us, and let us run with endurance the race that is set before us.

Hebrews 12:1 NKJV

Since we've compiled this long and sorry record as sinners (both us and them) and proved that we are utterly incapable of living the glorious lives God wills for us, God did it for us. Out of sheer generosity he put us in right standing with himself. A pure gift. He got us out of the mess we're in and restored us to where he always wanted us to be. And he did it by means of Jesus Christ.

Romans 3:23 MSG

All who indulge in a sinful life are dangerously lawless, for sin is a major disruption of God's order.

1 John 3:4 MSG

SUMMING IT UP

Sexual immorality is a sin that has the power to destroy the things you hold dear, starting, of course, with your family. So you must never let down your guard.

PART 3

GUARD YOUR STEPS

GUARD YOUR STEPS BY MAKING A STRAIGHT PATH

Mark out a straight path for your feet;
then stick to the path and stay safe.

Proverbs 4:26 NLT

I f you desire to guard your heart, you must choose a path that is pleasing to God, but you'll be tempted to choose a different path. If you're like most people, you seek the admiration of your neighbors, your coworkers, and your family members. But the eagerness to please others should never overshadow your eagerness to please God. If you seek to fulfill the purposes that God has in store for you, then you must be a "doer of the word." And how can you do so? By putting God first.

The words of Matthew 6:33 make it clear: "But seek first the kingdom of God and His righteousness, and all these things will be provided for you" (Holman CSB). God has given you a priceless guidebook, an indispensable tool for "seeking His kingdom." That tool, of course, is the Holy Bible. It contains thorough instructions which, if followed, lead to fulfillment, righteousness, and salvation.

But for those who would ignore God's Word, Martin Luther issued this stern warning: "You may as well quit reading and hearing the Word of God and give it to the devil if you do not desire to live according to it." Luther understood that obedience leads to abundance just as surely as disobedience leads to disaster; you should understand it, too.

Each new day presents countless opportunities to put God in first place . . . or not. When you honor Him by living according to His commandments, you earn the abundance and peace that He promises. But, if you ignore God's teachings, you will inevitably bring needless suffering upon yourself and your family.

Would you like a time-tested formula for successful living? Here it is: Don't just listen to God's Word, live by it. Does this sound too simple? Perhaps it is simple, but it is also the only way to reap the marvelous riches that God has in store for you.

A Tip for Guarding Your Heart

Ask yourself if your behavior has been radically changed by your unfolding relationship with God. If the answer to this question is unclear to you—or if the honest answer is a resounding no—think of a single step you can take, a positive change in your life, that will bring you closer to your Creator.

WORDS OF WISDOM

Discrepancies between values and practices create chaos in a person's life.

John Maxwell

Obedience is the outward expression of your love of God.

Henry Blackaby

There may be no trumpet sound or loud applause when we make a right decision, just a calm sense of resolution and peace.

Gloria Gaither

No more duty can be urged upon those who are entering the great theater of life than simple loyalty to their best convictions.

Edwin Hubbel Chapin

Do nothing that you would not like to be doing when Jesus comes. Go no place where you would not like to be found when He returns.

Corrie ten Boom

GOD'S WORDS OF WISDOM

In everything set them an example by doing what is good.

Titus 2:7 NIV

Are there those among you who are truly wise and understanding? Then they should show it by living right and doing good things with a gentleness that comes from wisdom.

James 3:13 NCV

Even a child is known by his actions, by whether his conduct is pure and right.

Proverbs 20:11 NIV

Here is a simple, rule-of-thumb for behavior: Ask yourself what you want people to do for you, then grab the initiative and do it for them. Add up God's Law and Prophets and this is what you get.

Matthew 7:12 MSG

Light shines on the godly, and joy on those who do right. May all who are godly be happy in the Lord and praise his holy name.

Psalm 97:11-12 NLT

SUMMING IT UP

How can you guard your steps? By walking with Jesus every day of your life.

GUARD YOUR STEPS BY ASKING GOD

So I say to you, keep asking, and it will be given to you.
Keep searching, and you will find.
Keep knocking, and the door will be opened to you.

Luke 11:9 Holman CSB

I f you sincerely want to guard your heart, you should ask for God's help. How often do you ask God for His help and His wisdom? Occasionally? Intermittently? Whenever you experience a crisis? Hopefully not. Hopefully, you've acquired the habit of asking for God's assistance early and often. And hopefully, you have learned to seek His guidance in every aspect of your life.

Jesus made it clear to His disciples: they should petition God to meet their needs. So should you. Genuine, heartfelt prayer produces powerful changes in you and in your world. When you lift your heart to God, you open yourself to a never-ending source of divine wisdom and infinite love.

God can do great things through you if you have the courage to ask Him (and the determination to keep asking Him). But don't expect Him to do all the work. When you do your part, He will do His part—and when He does, you can expect miracles to happen.

The Bible promises that God will guide you if you let Him. Your job is to let Him. But sometimes, you will be tempted to do otherwise. Sometimes, you'll be tempted to go along with the crowd; other times, you'll be tempted to do things your way, not God's way. When you feel those temptations, resist them.

God has promised that when you ask for His help, He will not withhold it. So ask. Ask Him to meet the needs of your day. Ask Him to lead you, to protect you, and to correct you. Then, trust the answers He gives.

God stands at the door and waits. When you knock, He opens. When you ask, He answers. Your task, of course, is to make God a full partner in every aspect of your life—and to seek His guidance prayerfully, confidently, and often.

Until now you have not asked for anything in my name. Ask and you will receive, so that your joy will be the fullest possible joy.

John 16:24 NCV

A TIP FOR GUARDING YOUR HEART

If you want more from life, ask more from God. If you seek any other worthy goal, ask God (and keep asking Him) until He answers your prayers.

WORDS OF WISDOM

All we have to do is to acknowledge our need, move from self-sufficiency to dependence, and ask God to become our hiding place.

Bill Hybels

Some people think God does not like to be troubled with our constant asking. But, the way to trouble God is not to come at all.

D. L. Moody

Don't be afraid to ask your heavenly Father for anything you need. Indeed, nothing is too small for God's attention or too great for his power.

Dennis Swanberg

There is a communion with God that asks for nothing, yet asks for everything . . . He who seeks the Father more than anything he can give is likely to have what he asks, for he is not likely to ask amiss.

George MacDonald

When will we realize that we're not troubling God with our questions and concerns? His heart is open to hear us—his touch nearer than our next thought—as if no one in the world existed but us. Our very personal God wants to hear from us personally.

Gigi Graham Tchividjian

GOD'S WORDS OF WISDOM

If you need wisdom—if you want to know what God wants you to do—ask him, and he will gladly tell you. He will not resent your asking.

James 1:5 NLT

From now on, whatever you request along the lines of who I am and what I am doing, I'll do it. That's how the Father will be seen for who he is in the Son. I mean it. Whatever you request in this way, I'll do.

John 14:13-14 MSG

You did not choose me, but I chose you and appointed you to go and bear fruit—fruit that will last. Then the Father will give you whatever you ask in my name.

John 15:16 NIV

You fathers—if your children ask for a fish, do you give them a snake instead? Or if they ask for an egg, do you give them a scorpion? Of course not! If you sinful people know how to give good gifts to your children, how much more will your heavenly Father give the Holy Spirit to those who ask him.

Luke 11:11-13 NLT

SUMMING IT UP

If you sincerely want to guard your steps, ask for God's help.

GUARD YOUR STEPS AGAINST EVIL

Don't get sidetracked; keep your feet from following evil.

Proverbs 4:27 NLT

This world is God's creation, and it contains the wonderful fruits of His handiwork. But, the world also contains countless opportunities to stray from God's will. Temptations are everywhere, and the devil, it seems, never takes a day off. Our task, as believers, is to turn away from temptation and to place our lives squarely in the center of God's will.

In his letter to Jewish Christians, Peter offered a stern warning: "Your adversary, the devil, prowls around like a roaring lion, seeking someone to devour" (I Peter 5:8 NASB). What was true in New Testament times is equally true in our own. Evil is indeed abroad in the world, and Satan continues to sow the seeds of destruction far and wide. In a very real sense, our world is at war: good versus evil, sin versus righteousness, hope versus suffering, praise versus apathy. As Christians, we must ensure that we place ourselves squarely on the right side of these conflicts: God's side. How can we do it? By thoughtfully studying God's Word, by regularly worshiping with fellow believers, and by guarding our hearts and minds against the subtle temptations of the enemy. When we do these things, we are protected.

Are you determined to stand up against evil whenever and wherever you confront it? And are you fully prepared to distance yourself from the countless temptations that have become so thoroughly woven into the fabric of society. If so, congratulations. That means you're an active-duty participant in the battle against a powerful and dangerous adversary. And with God's help, you're destined to win the battle *and* the war.

We are in a continual battle
with the spiritual forces of evil,
but we will triumph when we yield
to God's leading and call
on His powerful presence in prayer.

Shirley Dobson

A TIP FOR GUARDING YOUR HEART

There is darkness in this world, but God's light can overpower any darkness.

WORDS OF WISDOM

Our evil comes from our lack of resemblance to God and ignorance of Him. On the other hand, our great good consists in our resemblance of Him.

St. Methodius of Olympus

We need not despair of any man so long as he lives. For God deemed it better to bring good out of evil than not to permit evil at all.

St. Augustine

Christianity isn't a religion about going to Sunday school, potluck suppers, being nice, holding car washes, sending your secondhand clothes off to Mexico—as good as those things might be. This is a world at war.

John Eldredge

The only thing necessary for the triumph of evil is for good men to do nothing.

Edmund Burke

GOD'S WORDS OF WISDOM

Therefore, submit to God. But resist the Devil, and he will flee from you. Draw near to God, and He will draw near to you. Cleanse your hands, sinners, and purify your hearts, double-minded people!

James 4:7-8 Holman CSB

This High Priest of ours understands our weaknesses, for he faced all of the same temptations we do, yet he did not sin.

Hebrews 4:15 NLT

Do not be conquered by evil, but conquer evil with good.

Romans 12:21 Holman CSB

Do not fret because of evildoers; don't envy the wicked.

Proverbs 24:19 NLT

SUMMING IT UP

Evil exists, and it exists someplace not too far from you. You must guard your steps and your heart accordingly.

GUARD YOUR STEPS BY OBEYING GOD'S COMMANDMENTS

Here is my final conclusion: Fear God and obey his commands,
for this is the duty of every person.

Ecclesiastes 12:13 NLT

Y ou guard your steps whenever you are obedient to God. And make no mistake—obedience is determined, not by words, but by deeds. Talking about righteousness is easy; living righteously is far more difficult, especially in today's temptation-filled world.

Since God created Adam and Eve, we human beings have been rebelling against our Creator. Why? Because we are unwilling to trust God's Word, and we are unwilling to follow His commandments. God has given us a guidebook for righteous living called the Holy Bible. It contains thorough instructions which, if followed, lead to fulfillment, abundance, and salvation. But, if we choose to ignore God's commandments, the results are as predictable as they are tragic.

In Ephesians 2:10 we read, "For we are His workmanship, created in Christ Jesus for good works." (NKJV). These words are instructive: We are not saved by good works, but for good works. Good works are not the root, but rather the fruit of our salvation.

When we seek righteousness in our own lives—and when we seek the companionship of those who do likewise—we reap the spiritual rewards that God intends for our lives. When we behave ourselves as godly men and women, we honor God. When we live righteously and according to God's commandments, He blesses us in ways that we cannot fully understand.

Do you seek God's peace and His blessings? Then obey Him. When you're faced with a difficult choice or a powerful temptation, seek God's counsel and trust the counsel He gives. Invite God into your heart and live according to His commandments. When you do, you will be blessed today, and tomorrow, and forever.

Peter and the other apostles replied:
"We must obey God rather than men!"

Acts 5:29 NIV

A TIP FOR GUARDING YOUR HEART

Obedience leads to spiritual growth. Oswald Chambers correctly observed, "We grow spiritually as our Lord grew physically: by a life of simple, unobtrusive obedience."

WORDS OF WISDOM

The cross that Jesus commands you and me to carry is the cross of submissive obedience to the will of God, even when His will includes suffering and hardship and things we don't want to do.

Anne Graham Lotz

True faith commits us to obedience.

A. W. Tozer

You may not always see immediate results, but all God wants is your obedience and faithfulness.

Vonette Bright

I don't always like His decisions, but when I choose to obey Him, the act of obedience still "counts" with Him even if I'm not thrilled about it.

Beth Moore

Trials and sufferings teach us to obey the Lord by faith, and we soon learn that obedience pays off in joyful ways.

Bill Bright

GOD'S WORDS OF WISDOM

*It is the L*ORD *your God you must follow, and him you must revere.*
Keep his commands and obey him; serve him and hold fast to him.

Deuteronomy 13:4 NIV

The world and its desires pass away, but the man who does the will of
God lives forever.

1 John 2:17 NIV

So roll up your sleeves, put your mind in gear, be totally ready to
receive the gift that's coming when Jesus arrives. Don't lazily slip back
into those old grooves of evil, doing just what you feel like doing. You
didn't know any better then; you do now.

1 Peter 1:13-15 MSG

*Does the L*ORD *delight in burnt offerings and sacrifices as much as in*
*obeying the voice of the L*ORD*? To obey is better than sacrifice . . . .*

1 Samuel 15:22 NIV

SUMMING IT UP

God has rules. When we follow them, we are blessed; when
we ignore them, we are harmed.

GUARD YOUR STEPS WITH GODLY FRIENDS

As iron sharpens iron, a friend sharpens a friend.

Proverbs 27:17 NLT

Make no mistake: your friends can help you guard your steps—and it's up to you to let them.

The dictionary defines the word "friend" as "a person who is attached to another by feelings of affection or personal regard." This definition is accurate, as far as it goes, but when we examine the deeper meaning of friendship, many more descriptors come to mind: trustworthiness, loyalty, helpfulness, kindness, understanding, forgiveness, encouragement, humor, and cheerfulness, to mention but a few. Needless to say, our trusted friends and family members can help us discover God's unfolding purposes for our lives. Our task is to enlist our friends' wisdom, their cooperation, their honesty, and their encouragement.

As you consider the many blessings that God has given you, remember to thank Him for the friends He has chosen to place along your path. Seek their guidance, and, when asked, never withhold yours. Then, as you travel through life with trusted companions by your side, you will bless them, and they will richly bless you.

Loyal Christian friendship is ordained by God. Throughout the Bible, we are reminded to love one another, to care for one another, and to treat one another as we wish to be treated. So remember the important role that Christian friendship plays in God's plans for His kingdom and for your life. Resolve to be a trustworthy, loyal friend. And, treasure the people in your life who are loyal friends to you. Friendship is, after all, a glorious gift, praised by God. Give thanks for that gift and nurture it.

In friendship, God opens your eyes
to the glories of Himself.

Joni Eareckson Tada

A TIP FOR GUARDING YOUR HEART

Today, as you think about the nature and the quality of your friendships, remember the first rule of making (and keeping) friends: it's the Golden Rule, and it starts like this: "Do unto others . . . ."

WORDS OF WISDOM

Though I know intellectually how vulnerable I am to pride and power, I am the last one to know when I succumb to their seduction. That's why spiritual Lone Rangers are so dangerous—and why we must depend on trusted brothers and sisters who love us enough to tell us the truth.

Chuck Colson

Friendships are living organisms at work. They continue to unfold, change, and emerge.

Barbara Johnson

The glory of friendship is not the outstretched hand, or the kindly smile, or the joy of companionship. It is the spiritual inspiration that comes to one when he discovers that someone else believes in him and is willing to trust him with his friendship.

Corrie ten Boom

You can make more friends in two months by becoming more interested in other people than you can in two years by trying to get other people interested in you.

Dale Carnegie

GOD'S WORDS OF WISDOM

Beloved, if God so loved us, we also ought to love one another.

1 John 4:11 NKJV

Greater love has no one than this, that he lay down his life for his friends.

John 15:13 NIV

I thank my God upon every remembrance of you.

Philippians 1:3 NKJV

A friend loves at all times, and a brother is born for adversity.

Proverbs 17:17 NIV

Finally, all of you be of one mind, having compassion for one another; love as brothers, be tenderhearted, be courteous.

1 Peter 3:8 NKJV

SUMMING IT UP

Thank your Creator God for the godly friends He has placed along your path. Cherish those friendships, and do your best to make them flourish.

GUARD YOUR STEPS WITH A DAILY DEVOTIONAL

*Morning by morning he wakens me and
opens my understanding to his will.
The Sovereign Lord has spoken to me, and I have listened.*

Isaiah 50:4-5 NLT

E ach day has 1,440 minutes—do you value your relationship with God enough to spend a few of those minutes with Him? He deserves that much of your time and more—is He receiving it from you? Hopefully so. But if you find that you're simply "too busy" for a daily chat with your Father in heaven, it's time to take a long, hard look at your priorities and your values.

As you consider your plans for the day ahead, here's a tip: organize your life around this simple principle: "God first." When you place your Creator where He belongs—at the very center of your day and your life—the rest of your priorities will fall into place.

Each new day is a gift from God, and if you are wise, you will spend a few quiet moments each morning thanking the

Giver. Daily life is woven together with the threads of habit, and no habit is more important to your spiritual health than the discipline of daily prayer and devotion to the Creator.

Warren Wiersbe writes, "Surrender your mind to the Lord at the beginning of each day." And that's sound advice. When you begin each day with your head bowed and your heart lifted, you are reminded of God's love, His protection, and His commandments. Then, you can align your priorities for the coming day with the teachings and commandments that God has placed upon your heart.

So, if you've acquired the unfortunate habit of trying to "squeeze" God into the corners of your life, it's time to reshuffle the items on your to-do list by placing God first. God wants your undivided attention, not the leftovers of your day. And if you haven't already done so, form the habit of spending quality time with your Father in heaven. He deserves it . . . and so, for that matter, do you.

A TIP FOR GUARDING YOUR HEART

To guard your heart—and to seek God's guidance—you must begin each day with a time of quiet reflection, Bible study, and prayer.

WORDS OF WISDOM

God is a place of safety you can run to, but it helps if you are running to Him on a daily basis so that you are in familiar territory.

Stormie Omartian

What digestion is to the body, meditation is to the soul.

Warren Wiersbe

God calls us to seek him daily in order to serve him daily.

Sheila Cragg

A quiet morning with a loving God puts the events of the upcoming day into proper perspective.

Janette Oke

If we really believe not only that God exists but also that God is actively present in our lives—healing, teaching, and guiding—we need to set aside a time and space to give God our undivided attention.

Henri Nouwen

GOD'S WORDS OF WISDOM

You will be a good servant of Christ Jesus, constantly nourished on the words of the faith and of the sound doctrine which you have been following.

1 Timothy 4:6 NASB

But grow in the grace and knowledge of our Lord and Savior Jesus Christ. To Him be the glory both now and forever. Amen.

2 Peter 3:18 NKJV

There's nothing like the written Word of God for showing you the way to salvation through faith in Christ Jesus. Every part of Scripture is God-breathed and useful one way or another, showing us truth, exposing our rebellion, correcting our mistakes, training us to live God's way. Through the Word we are put together and shaped up for the tasks God has for us.

2 Timothy 3:15-17 MSG

For I am not ashamed of the gospel of Christ, for it is the power of God to salvation for everyone who believes.

Romans 1:16 NKJV

SUMMING IT UP

You need a regular appointment with your Creator. God is ready to talk to you, and you should prepare yourself each morning to talk to Him.

GUARD YOUR STEPS WITH WISDOM

How much better to get wisdom than gold!
And to get understanding is to be chosen rather than silver.

Proverbs 16:16 NKJV

Do you place a high value on the acquisition of wisdom? If so, you are not alone; most people would like to be wise, but not everyone is willing to do the work that is required to become wise. Wisdom is not like a mushroom; it does not spring up overnight. It is, instead, like an oak tree that starts as a tiny acorn, grows into a sapling, and eventually reaches up to the sky, tall and strong.

To become wise, you must seek God's guidance and live according to His Word. To become wise, you must seek instruction with consistency and purpose. To become wise, you must not only learn the lessons of the Christian life, but you must also live by them. But oftentimes, that's easier said than done.

Sometimes, amid the demands of daily life, you will lose perspective. Life may seem out of balance, and the pressures of everyday living may seem overwhelming. What's needed is a fresh perspective, a restored sense of balance . . . and God's wisdom. If you call upon the Lord and seek to see the world through His eyes, He will give you guidance, wisdom and perspective. When you make God's priorities your priorities, He will lead you according to His plan and according to His commandments. When you study God's teachings, you are reminded that God's reality is the ultimate reality.

Do you really want to guard your heart? If so, you must study the ultimate source of wisdom: the Word of God. You must seek out worthy mentors and listen carefully to their advice. You must associate, day in and day out, with godly men and women. Then, as you accumulate wisdom, you must not keep it for yourself; you must, instead, share it with your friends and family members.

But be forewarned: if you sincerely seek to share your hard-earned wisdom with others, your actions must reflect the values that you hold dear. The best way to share your wisdom—perhaps the only way—is not by your words, but by your example.

Happy is the person who finds wisdom,
the one who gets understanding.

Proverbs 3:13 NCV

A TIP FOR GUARDING YOUR HEART

Simply put, wisdom starts with God. If you don't have God's wisdom—and if you don't live according to God's rules— you'll pay a big price later.

WORDS OF WISDOM

Wisdom is knowledge applied. Head knowledge is useless on the battlefield. Knowledge stamped on the heart makes one wise.

Beth Moore

God's plan for our guidance is for us to grow gradually in wisdom before we get to the crossroads.

Bill Hybels

When you and I are related to Jesus Christ, our strength and wisdom and peace and joy and love and hope may run out, but His life rushes in to keep us filled to the brim. We are showered with blessings, not because of anything we have or have not done, but simply because of Him.

Anne Graham Lotz

Most of us go through life praying a little, planning a little, jockeying for position, hoping but never being quite certain of anything, and always secretly afraid that we will miss the way. This is a tragic waste of truth and never gives rest to the heart. There is a better way. It is to repudiate our own wisdom and take instead the infinite wisdom of God.

A. W. Tozer

Knowledge is horizontal. Wisdom is vertical; it comes down from above.

Billy Graham

GOD'S WORDS OF WISDOM

The Lord says, "I will make you wise and show you where to go. I will guide you and watch over you."

Psalm 32:8 NCV

Wisdom is the principal thing; therefore get wisdom. And in all your getting, get understanding.

Proverbs 4:7 NKJV

Anyone who listens to my teaching and obeys me is wise, like a person who builds a house on solid rock. Though the rain comes in torrents and the floodwaters rise and the winds beat against that house, it won't collapse, because it is built on rock.

Matthew 7:24–25 NLT

But the wisdom that is from above is first pure, then peaceable, gentle, willing to yield, full of mercy and good fruits, without partiality and without hypocrisy.

James 3:17 NKJV

SUMMING IT UP

God makes His wisdom available to you. Your job is to acknowledge, to understand, and (above all) to use that wisdom.

GUARD YOUR STEPS WITH FELLOWSHIP

You must get along with each other.
You must learn to be considerate of one another,
cultivating a life in common.

1 Corinthians 1:10 MSG

Y ou can guard your steps by associating yourself with a faithful group of fellow believers—and that's precisely what you should do. Your association with fellow Christians should be uplifting, enlightening, encouraging, and consistent. In short, fellowship with other believers should be an integral part of your everyday life.

When you make a habit of spending time with like-minded believers, you'll enhance your own life, and theirs. Plus, you'll be protecting yourself (and them) against the inevitable temptations and distractions that have become so commonplace in our modern society. So what are you waiting for? The answer, of course, is that you shouldn't wait another minute . . . you should reach out to your brothers and sisters in Christ, starting right now. And you should keep reaching out as long as you live.

Are you an active member of your own fellowship? Are you a builder of bridges inside the four walls of your church and outside it? Do you contribute to God's glory by sharing your time and your talents with a close-knit band of believers? Hopefully so. The fellowship of believers is intended to be a powerful tool for spreading God's Good News and uplifting His children. God intends for you to be a fully contributing member of that fellowship. Your intentions should be the same.

Don't become partners with those who reject God.
How can you make a partnership
out of right and wrong? That's not partnership;
that's war. Is light best friends with dark?

2 Corinthians 6:14 MSG

A TIP FOR GUARDING YOUR HEART

Christians are not Lone Rangers. They are members of a spiritual family, and they need one another.

WORDS OF WISDOM

A vibrant fellowship of believers is one of our greatest apologetics for the truth of the gospel.

Stanley Grenz

Unity is the soul of fellowship. Destroy it, and you rip the heart out of Christ's Body.

Rick Warren

In God's economy you will be hard-pressed to find many examples of successful "Lone Rangers."

Luci Swindoll

The Bible knows nothing of solitary religion.

John Wesley

Mutual love produces the harmony that's conducive to spiritual stability and reflects what the church is all about: supporting the weak, lifting the fallen, and restoring the broken.

John MacArthur

GOD'S WORDS OF WISDOM

Don't you realize that all of you together are the temple of God and that the Spirit of God lives in you?

1 Corinthians 3:16 NLT

He keeps us in step with each other. His very breath and blood flow through us, nourishing us so that we will grow up healthy in God, robust in love.

Ephesians 4:16 MSG

You can develop a healthy, robust community that lives right with God and enjoy its results only if you do the hard work of getting along with each other, treating each other with dignity and honor.

James 3:18 MSG

To turn from evil is understanding.

Job 28:28 Holman CSB

SUMMING IT UP

You need fellowship with men and women of faith. And your Christian friends need fellowship with you. So what are you waiting for?

GUARD YOUR STEPS BY PLANNING WISELY

The plans of the diligent certainly lead to profit,
but anyone who is reckless only becomes poor.

Proverbs 21:5 Holman CSB

Are you willing to plan for the future—and are you willing to work diligently to accomplish the plans that you've made? If you desire to reap a bountiful harvest from life, you should plan for the future (by crafting a "to-do list for life") while entrusting the final outcome to God. Then, you should do your part to make the future better (by working dutifully), while acknowledging the sovereignty of God's hands over all affairs, including your own.

As you make plans and establish priorities, remember this: you're not the only one working on your behalf: God, too, is at work. And with Him as your partner, your ultimate success is guaranteed.

God has big plans for your life, wonderful, surprising plans . . . but He won't force those plans upon you. To the contrary, He has given you free will, the ability to make decisions on your own. Now, it's up to you to make those decisions wisely.

If you seek to live in accordance with God's plan for your life, you will study His Word, you will be attentive to His instructions, and you will be watchful for His signs. You will associate with fellow believers who, by their words and actions, will encourage your spiritual growth. You will assiduously avoid those two terrible temptations: the temptation to sin and the temptation to squander time. And finally, you will listen carefully, even reverently, to the conscience that God has placed in your heart.

God intends to use you in wonderful, unexpected ways if you let Him. Your job, of course, is to let Him.

Commit to the Lord whatever you do,
and your plans will succeed.

Proverbs 16:3 NIV

A TIP FOR GUARDING YOUR HEART

Whose plans will you trust: yours or God's? The answer should be obvious. So as you plan for this day and for all the ones that follow it, plan carefully and prayerfully.

WORDS OF WISDOM

Allow your dreams a place in your prayers and plans. God-given dreams can help you move into the future He is preparing for you.

Barbara Johnson

Plan ahead—it wasn't raining when Noah built the ark.

Anonymous

Plan your work. Without a system, you'll feel swamped.

Norman Vincent Peale

God has a plan for your life . . . do you?

Jim Gallery

The only way you can experience abundant life is to surrender your plans to Him.

Charles Stanley

GOD'S WORDS OF WISDOM

May he give you the desire of your heart and make all your plans succeed.

Psalm 20:4 NIV

First plant your fields; then build your barn.

Proverbs 24:27 MSG

Plans fail for lack of counsel, but with many advisors, they succeed.

Proverbs 15:22 NIV

A prudent person foresees the danger ahead and takes precautions. The simpleton goes blindly on and suffers the consequences.

Proverbs 27:12 NLT

But the noble man makes noble plans, and by noble deeds he stands.

Isaiah 32:8 NIV

SUMMING IT UP

It isn't that complicated: If you plan your steps carefully, and if you follow your plan conscientiously, you will probably succeed. If you don't, you probably won't.

GUARD YOUR STEPS BY SETTING A GOOD EXAMPLE

Be an example to the believers in word,
in conduct, in love, in spirit, in faith, in purity.

1 Timothy 4:12 NKJV

Whether we like it or not, all of us are role models. Our friends and family members watch our actions and, as followers of Christ, we are obliged to act accordingly.

What kind of example are you? Are you the kind of person whose life serves as a genuine example of righteousness? Does your behavior serve as a positive role model for others? Are you the kind of believer whose actions, day in and day out, are based upon kindness, faithfulness, and a love for the Lord? If so, you are not only blessed by God, but you are also a powerful force for good in a world that desperately needs positive influences such as yours.

Phillips Brooks had simple advice for believers of every generation; he said, "Be such a person, and live such a life, that if every person were such as you, and every life a life like yours, this earth would be God's Paradise." And that's precisely the kind of Christian you should strive to be . . . but it isn't always easy.

You live in a dangerous, temptation-filled world. That's why you encounter so many opportunities to stray from God's commandments. Resist those temptations! When you do, you'll earn God's blessings, and you'll serve as a positive role model for your family and friends.

Corrie ten Boom advised, "Don't worry about what you do not understand. Worry about what you do understand in the Bible but do not live by." And that's sound advice because your families and friends are watching . . . and so, for that matter, is God.

In every way be an example of doing good deeds.
When you teach, do it with honesty and seriousness.

Titus 2:7 NCV

A Tip for Guarding Your Heart

As a Christian, the most important light you shine is the light that your own life shines on the lives of others. May your light shine brightly, righteously, obediently, and eternally!

WORDS OF WISDOM

You can never separate a leader's actions from his character.

John Maxwell

The sermon of your life in tough times ministers to people more powerfully than the most eloquent speaker.

Bill Bright

What we practice, not (save at rare intervals) what we preach, is usually our great contribution to the conversion of others.

C. S. Lewis

Our walk counts far more than our talk, always!

George Mueller

We urgently need people who encourage and inspire us to move toward God and away from the world's enticing pleasures.

Jim Cymbala

GOD'S WORDS OF WISDOM

We have around us many people whose lives tell us what faith means. So let us run the race that is before us and never give up. We should remove from our lives anything that would get in the way and the sin that so easily holds us back.

Hebrews 12:1 NCV

In everything you do, stay away from complaining and arguing, so that no one can speak a word of blame against you. You are to live clean, innocent lives as children of God in a dark world full of crooked and perverse people. Let your lives shine brightly before them.

Philippians 2:14-15 NLT

You are the light that gives light to the world. In the same way, you should be a light for other people. Live so that they will see the good things you do and will praise your Father in heaven.

Matthew 5:14,16 NCV

Do you want to be counted wise, to build a reputation for wisdom? Here's what you do: Live well, live wisely, live humbly. It's the way you live, not the way you talk, that counts.

James 3:13 MSG

SUMMING IT UP

God wants you to be a positive role model. And that's what you should want, too.

GUARD YOUR STEPS BY LIVING PURPOSEFULLY

You will show me the path of life; in Your presence is fullness of joy; at Your right hand are pleasures forevermore.

Psalm 16:11 NKJV

L ife is best lived on purpose, not by accident: the sooner we discover what God intends for us to do with our lives, the better. But God's purposes aren't always clear to us. Sometimes we wander aimlessly in a wilderness of our own making. And sometimes, we struggle mightily against God in a vain effort to find success and happiness through our own means, not His.

Whenever we struggle against God's plans, we suffer. When we resist God's calling, our efforts bear little fruit. Our best strategy, therefore, is to seek God's wisdom and to follow Him wherever He chooses to lead. When we do so, we are blessed.

When we align ourselves with God's purposes, we avail ourselves of His power and His peace. But how can we know precisely what God's intentions are? The answer, of course, is that even the most well-intentioned believers face periods of uncertainty and doubt about the direction of their lives. So, too, will you.

When you arrive at one of life's inevitable crossroads, that is precisely the moment when you should turn your thoughts and prayers toward God. When you do, He will make Himself known to you in a time and manner of His choosing.

Sometimes, God's intentions will be clear to you; other times, God's plan will seem uncertain at best. But even on those difficult days when you are unsure of which way to turn, you must never lose sight of these overriding facts: God created you for a reason; He has important work for you to do; and He's waiting patiently for you to do it. So why not begin today?

A TIP FOR GUARDING YOUR HEART

Discovering God's purpose for your life requires a willingness to be open. God's plan is unfolding day by day. If you keep your eyes and your heart open, He'll reveal His plans. God has big things in store for you, but He may have quite a few lessons to teach you before you are fully prepared to do His will and fulfill His purposes.

WORDS OF WISDOM

How much of our lives are, well, so daily. How often our hours are filled with the mundane, seemingly unimportant things that have to be done, whether at home or work. These very "daily" tasks could become a celebration of praise. "It is through consecration," someone has said, "that drudgery is made divine."

Gigi Graham Tchividjian

God is more concerned with the direction of your life than with its speed.

Marie T. Freeman

God specializes in things fresh and firsthand. His plans for you this year may outshine those of the past. He's prepared to fill your days with reasons to give Him praise.

Joni Eareckson Tada

Oh Lord, let me not live to be useless.

John Wesley

Without God, life has no purpose, and without purpose, life has no meaning.

Rick Warren

GOD'S WORDS OF WISDOM

Whatever you do, do all to the glory of God.

1 Corinthians 10:31 NKJV

You're sons of Light, daughters of Day. We live under wide open skies and know where we stand. So let's not sleepwalk through life . . .

1 Thessalonians 5:5-6 MSG

We look at this Son and see the God who cannot be seen. We look at this Son and see God's original purpose in everything created.

Colossians 1:15 MSG

To everything there is a season, a time for every purpose under heaven.

Ecclesiastes 3:1 NKJV

SUMMING IT UP

When you gain a clear vision of your purpose for life here on earth—and for life everlasting—your steps will be sure.

GUARD YOUR STEPS WITH WISE PRIORITIES

It's obvious, isn't it? The place where your treasure is,
is the place you will most want to be, and end up being.

Luke 12:34 MSG

O n your daily to-do list, all items are not created equal: Certain tasks are extremely important while others are not. Therefore, it's imperative that you prioritize your daily activities and complete each task in the approximate order of its importance.

The principle of doing first things first is simple in theory but more complicated in practice. Well-meaning family, friends, and coworkers have a way of making unexpected demands upon your time. Furthermore, each day has it own share of minor emergencies; these urgent matters tend to draw your attention away from more important ones. On paper, prioritizing is simple, but to act upon those priorities in the real world requires maturity, patience, determination, and balance.

If you fail to prioritize your day, life will automatically do the job for you. So your choice is simple: prioritize or be prioritized. It's a choice that will help determine the quality of your life.

If you're having trouble balancing the many demands of everyday living, perhaps you've been trying to organize your life according to your own plans, not God's. A better strategy, of course, is to take your daily obligations and place them in the hands of the One who created you. To do so, you must prioritize your day according to God's commandments, and you must seek His will and His wisdom in all matters. Then, you can face the coming day with the assurance that the same God who created our universe out of nothingness will help you place first things first in your own life.

Are you living a balanced life that allows time for worship, for family, for work, for exercise, and a little time left over for you? Or do you feel overworked, under-appreciated, overwhelmed, and underpaid? If your to-do list is "maxed out" and your energy is on the wane, it's time to restore a sense of balance to your life. You can do so by turning the concerns and the priorities of this day over to God—prayerfully, earnestly, and often. Then, you must listen for His answer . . . and trust the answer He gives.

A TIP FOR GUARDING YOUR HEART

Setting priorities may mean saying no. You don't have time to do everything, so it's perfectly okay to say no to the things that mean less, so that you'll have time for the things that mean more.

WORDS OF WISDOM

Getting things accomplished isn't nearly as important as taking time for love.

Janette Oke

Have you prayed about your resources lately? Find out how God wants you to use your time and your money. No matter what it costs, forsake all that is not of God.

Kay Arthur

Forgetting your mission leads, inevitably, to getting tangled up in details—details that can take you completely off your path.

Laurie Beth Jones

I have decided not to let my time be used up by people to whom I make no difference while I neglect those for whom I am irreplaceable.

Tony Campolo

Whole-life stewardship means putting the purposes of God at the very center of our lives and families.

Tom Sine

GOD'S WORDS OF WISDOM

*First pay attention to me, and then relax. Now you can take it
easy—you're in good hands.*

Proverbs 1:33 MSG

*And I pray this: that your love will keep on growing in knowledge
and every kind of discernment, so that you can determine what really
matters and can be pure and blameless in the day of Christ.*

Philippians 1:9 Holman CSB

*He said to them all, "If anyone desires to come after Me, let him deny
himself, and take up his cross daily, and follow Me. For whoever
desires to save his life will lose it, but whoever loses his life for My
sake will save it."*

Luke 9:23-24 NKJV

*Let us fix our eyes on Jesus, the author and perfecter of our faith,
who for the joy set before him endured the cross, scorning its shame,
and sat down at the right hand of the throne of God.*

Hebrews 12:2 NIV

SUMMING IT UP

The priorities you choose will dictate the life you live. So
choose carefully.

GUARD YOUR STEPS AGAINST PEER PRESSURE

Dear friend, don't let this bad example influence you.
Follow only what is good. Remember that those who do good
prove that they are God's children,
and those who do evil prove that they do not know God.

3 John 1:11 NLT

Whom will you try to please today: God or man? Your primary obligation, of course, is please your Father in heaven, not your friends in the neighborhood. But even if you're a devoted Christian, you may, from time to time, feel the urge to impress your peers—and sometimes that urge can be strong.

Peer pressure can be a good thing or a bad thing, depending upon your peers. If your peers encourage you to follow God's will and to obey His commandments, then you'll experience positive peer pressure, and that's good. But, if you are involved with friends who encourage you to do foolish things, you're facing a different kind of peer pressure . . . and you'd better beware. When you feel pressured to do things—or to say things—that lead you away from God, you're aiming straight for trouble. So don't do the "easy" thing or the "popular" thing. Do the right thing, and don't worry about winning popularity contests. Here are a few things to remember about peer pressure: 1. Peer pressure exists, and you may experience it at any age. 2. If your peers encourage you to behave yourself, to honor God, and to become a better person, peer pressure can actually be a good thing . . . up to a point. But remember: you don't have to be perfect to be wonderful. So if you're trying to be perfect, lighten up on yourself, and while you're at it, lighten up on others, too. 3. If your friends are encouraging you to misbehave or underachieve, find new friends. Today.

Rick Warren correctly observed, "Those who follow the crowd usually get lost in it." Are you satisfied to follow that crowd? If so, you will probably pay a heavy price for your shortsightedness. But if you're determined to follow the One from Galilee, He will guide your steps and bless your undertakings. To sum it up, here's your choice: you can choose to please God first, or you can fall prey to peer pressure. The choice is yours—and so are the consequences.

A TIP FOR GUARDING YOUR HEART

A thoughtful Christian doesn't follow the crowd . . . a thoughtful Christian follows Jesus.

WORDS OF WISDOM

There is nothing that makes more cowards and feeble men than public opinion.

Henry Ward Beecher

You will get untold flak for prioritizing God's revealed and present will for your life over man's . . . but, boy, is it worth it.

Beth Moore

Comparison is the root of all feelings of inferiority.

James Dobson

We, as God's people, are not only to stay far away from sin and sinners who would entice us, but we are to be so like our God that we mourn over sin.

Kay Arthur

Don't be addicted to approval. Follow your heart. Do what you believe God is telling you to do, and stand firm in Him and Him alone.

Joyce Meyer

GOD'S WORDS OF WISDOM

Do not be misled: "Bad company corrupts good character."

1 Corinthians 15:33 NIV

If you decide for God, living a life of God-worship, it follows that you don't fuss about what's on the table at mealtimes or whether the clothes in your closet are in fashion. There is far more to your life than the food you put in your stomach, more to your outer appearance than the clothes you hang on your body.

Matthew 6:25 MSG

We must obey God rather than men.

Acts 5:29 Holman CSB

My son, if sinners entice you, don't be persuaded.

Proverbs 1:10 Holman CSB

Blessed is the man who walks not in the counsel of the ungodly, nor stands in the path of sinners, nor sits in the seat of the scornful; but his delight is in the law of the Lord, and in His law he meditates day and night.

Psalm 1:1-2 NKJV

SUMMING IT UP

A great way to guard your steps is by associating with friends who guard theirs.

GUARD YOUR STEPS BY USING GOD'S GIFTS

Do not neglect the gift that is in you.

1 Timothy 4:14 Holman CSB

A ll of us have special talents, and you are no exception. But your talent is no guarantee of success; it must be cultivated and nurtured; otherwise, it will go unused . . . and God's gift to you will be squandered.

In the 25th chapter of Matthew, Jesus tells the "Parable of the Talents." In it, He describes a master who leaves his servants with varying amounts of money (talents). When the master returns, some servants have put their money to work and earned more, to which the master responds, "Well done, good and faithful servant! You have been faithful with a few things; I will put you in charge of many things. Come and share your master's happiness!" (Matthew 25:21 NIV)

But the story does not end so happily for the foolish servant who was given a single talent but did nothing with it. For this man, the master has nothing but reproach: "You wicked, lazy servant . . . ." (Matthew 25:26 NIV) The message from Jesus is clear: We must use our talents, not waste them.

Your particular talent is a treasure on temporary loan from God. He intends that your talent enrich the world and enrich your life. Value the gift that God has given you, nourish it, make it grow, and share it with the world. Then, when you meet your Master face-to-face, you, too, will hear those wonderful words, "Well done, good and faithful servant! . . . Come and share your Master's happiness!"

I remind you to fan into flame the gift of God.

2 Timothy 1:6 NIV

A TIP FOR GUARDING YOUR HEART

You are the sole owner of your own set of talents and opportunities. God has given you your own particular gifts— the rest is up to you.

WORDS OF WISDOM

God has given you special talents—now it's your turn to give them back to God.

Marie T. Freeman

Employ whatever God has entrusted you with, in doing good, all possible good, in every possible kind and degree.

John Wesley

If you want to reach your potential, you need to add a strong work ethic to your talent.

John Maxwell

Not everyone possesses boundless energy or a conspicuous talent. We are not equally blessed with great intellect or physical beauty or emotional strength. But we have all been given the same ability to be faithful.

Gigi Graham Tchividjian

God often reveals His direction for our lives through the way He made us . . . with a certain personality and unique skills.

Bill Hybels

GOD'S WORDS OF WISDOM

God has given gifts to each of you from his great variety of spiritual gifts. Manage them well so that God's generosity can flow through you.

1 Peter 4:10 NLT

Now there are varieties of gifts, but the same Spirit. And there are varieties of ministries, and the same Lord.

1 Corinthians 12:4-5 NASB

Every good gift and every perfect gift is from above, and cometh down from the Father of lights.

James 1:17 KJV

We have different gifts, according to the grace given us. If a man's gift is prophesying, let him use it in proportion to his faith. If it is serving, let him serve; if it is teaching, let him teach; if it is encouraging, let him encourage; if it is contributing to the needs of others, let him give generously; if it is leadership, let him govern diligently; if it is showing mercy, let him do it cheerfully.

Romans 12:6-8 NIV

SUMMING IT UP

God has given you a unique array of talents and opportunities. The rest is up to you.

GUARD YOUR STEPS BY MAKING SERVICE A HIGH PRIORITY

*Jesus sat down and called the twelve apostles to him.
He said, "Whoever wants to be the most important
must be last of all and servant of all."*

Mark 9:35 NCV

I f you genuinely seek to discover God's unfolding priorities for your life, you must ask yourself this question: "How does God want me to serve others?"

Whatever your path, whatever your calling, you may be certain of this: service to others is an integral part of God's plan for your life. Christ was the ultimate servant, the Savior who gave His life for mankind. As His followers, we, too, must become humble servants.

As Christians, we are instructed to serve others. But, as weak human beings, we sometimes fall short as we seek to puff ourselves up and glorify our own accomplishments. Jesus commands otherwise. He teaches us that the most esteemed men and women are not the self-congratulatory leaders of society but are instead the humblest of servants.

Are you willing to become a humble servant for Christ? Are you willing to roll up your sleeves and do your part to make the world a better place, or are you determined to keep all your blessings to yourself? The answer to these questions will determine the quantity and the quality of the service your render to God and to His children.

Today, you may feel the temptation to build yourself up in the eyes of your neighbors. Resist that temptation. Instead, serve your neighbors quietly and without fanfare. Find a need and fill it . . . humbly. Lend a helping hand and share a word of kindness . . . anonymously, for this is God's way.

As a humble servant, you will glorify yourself not before men, but before God, and that's what God intends. After all, earthly glory is fleeting: here today and all too soon gone. But, heavenly glory endures throughout eternity. So, the choice is yours: Either you can lift yourself up here on earth and be humbled in heaven, or vice versa. Choose vice versa.

A TIP FOR GUARDING YOUR HEART

Whatever your age, whatever your circumstances, you can serve: Each stage of life's journey is a glorious opportunity to place yourself in the service of the One who is the Giver of all blessings. As long as you live, you should honor God with your service to others.

WORDS OF WISDOM

Doing something positive toward another person is a practical approach to feeling good about yourself.

Barbara Johnson

If you want to discover your spiritual gifts, start obeying God. As you serve Him, you will find that He has given you the gifts that are necessary to follow through in obedience.

Anne Graham Lotz

We can never untangle all the woes in other people's lives. We can't produce miracles overnight. But we can bring a cup of cool water to a thirsty soul, or a scoop of laughter to a lonely heart.

Barbara Johnson

Have thy tools ready; God will find thee work.

Charles Kingsley

You can judge how far you have risen in the scale of life by asking one question: How wisely and how deeply do I care? To be Christianized is to be sensitized. Christians are people who care.

E. Stanley Jones

GOD'S WORDS OF WISDOM

So prepare your minds for service and have self-control.

1 Peter 1:13 NCV

Therefore, since we receive a kingdom which cannot be shaken, let us show gratitude, by which we may offer to God an acceptable service with reverence and awe . . . .

Hebrews 12:28 NASB

Suppose a brother or a sister is without clothes and daily food. If one of you says to him, "Go, I wish you well; keep warm and well fed," but does nothing about his physical needs, what good is it?

James 2:15-16 NIV

But a Samaritan, as he traveled, came where the man was; and when he saw him, he took pity on him. He went to him and bandaged his wounds, pouring on oil and wine. Then he put the man on his own donkey, took him to an inn and took care of him.

Luke 10:33-34 NIV

SUMMING IT UP

The direction of your steps and the quality of your life will be determined by the level of your service.

GUARD YOUR STEPS WITH YOUR FAMILY

Choose for yourselves today the one you will worship . . . .
As for me and my family, we will worship the Lord.

Joshua 24:15 Holman CSB

A loving family is a treasure from God. If God has blessed you with a close knit, supportive clan, offer a word of thanks to your Creator because He has given you one of His most precious earthy possessions. Your obligation, in response to God's gift, is to treat your family in ways that are consistent with His commandments.

You live in a fast-paced, demanding world, a place where life can be difficult and pressures can be intense. As those pressures build, you may tend to focus so intently upon your obligations that you lose sight, albeit temporarily, of your spiritual and emotional needs (that's one reason why a regular daily devotional time is so important; it offers a badly-needed dose of perspective).

Even when the demands of everyday life are great, you must never forget that you have been entrusted with a profound responsibility: the responsibility of contributing to your family's emotional and spiritual wellbeing. It's a big job, but with God's help, you're up to the task.

When you place God squarely in the center of your family's life—when you worship Him, praise Him, trust Him, and love Him—then He will most certainly bless you and yours in ways that you could have scarcely imagined.

So the next time your family life becomes a little stressful, remember this: That little band of men, women, kids, and babies is a priceless treasure on temporary loan from the Father above. And it's your responsibility to praise God for that gift—and to act accordingly.

Let love and faithfulness never leave you . . .
write them on the tablet of your heart.

Proverbs 3:3 NIV

A TIP FOR GUARDING YOUR HEART

If you're lucky enough to be a member of a loving, supportive family, then you owe it to yourself—and to them—to share your thoughts, your hopes, your encouragement, and your love.

WORDS OF WISDOM

When you think about it for a moment, it certainly makes sense that if people can establish a loving and compatible relationship at home, they have a better chance of establishing winning relationships with those with whom they work on a regular basis.

Zig Ziglar

Living life with a consistent spiritual walk deeply influences those we love most.

Vonette Bright

My primary role is not to be the boss and just look good, but to be a servant leader who enables and enhances my family to be their best.

Tim Hansel

Creating a warm, caring, supportive, encouraging environment is probably the most important thing you can do for your family.

Stephen Covey

When God asks someone to do something for Him entailing sacrifice, he makes up for it in surprising ways. Though He has led Bill all over the world to preach the gospel, He has not forgotten the little family in the mountains of North Carolina.

Ruth Bell Graham

GOD'S WORDS OF WISDOM

Love must be without hypocrisy. Detest evil; cling to what is good. Show family affection to one another with brotherly love. Outdo one another in showing honor.

Romans 12:9–10 Holman CSB

Their first responsibility is to show godliness at home and repay their parents by taking care of them. This is something that pleases God very much.

1 Timothy 5:4 NLT

Every kingdom divided against itself will be ruined, and every city or household divided against itself will not stand.

Matthew 12:25 NIV

If a kingdom is divided against itself, that kingdom cannot stand. If a house is divided against itself, that house cannot stand.

Mark 3:24-25 Holman CSB

SUMMING IT UP

Your family is a precious gift from above, a gift that should be treasured, nurtured, and loved.

GUARD YOUR STEPS BY SENSING GOD'S PRESENCE

Draw near to God, and He will draw near to you.

James 4:8 Holman CSB

In the quiet early morning, as the sun's first rays peak over the horizon, we may sense the presence of God. But as the day wears on and the demands of everyday life bear down upon us, we may become so wrapped up in earthy concerns that we forget to praise the Creator.

God is everywhere we have ever been and everywhere we will ever be. When we turn to Him often, we are blessed by His presence. But, if we ignore God's presence or rebel against it altogether, the world in which we live soon becomes a spiritual wasteland.

Since God is everywhere, we are free to sense His presence whenever we take the time to quiet our souls and turn our prayers to Him. But sometimes, amid the incessant demands of everyday life, we turn our thoughts far from God; when we do, we suffer.

Do you set aside quiet moments each day to offer praise to your Creator? You should. During these moments of stillness, you can sense the infinite love and power of our Lord. The familiar words of Psalm 46:10 remind us to "Be still, and know that I am God" (KJV). When we do so, we encounter the awesome presence of our loving Heavenly Father.

Are you tired, discouraged or fearful? Be comforted because God is with you. Are you confused? Listen to the quiet voice of your Heavenly Father. Are you bitter? Talk with God and seek His guidance. Are you celebrating a great victory? Thank God and praise Him. He is the Giver of all things good. In whatever condition you find yourself—whether you are happy or sad, victorious or vanquished, troubled or triumphant—celebrate God's presence. And be comforted in the knowledge that God is not just near. He is here.

No, I will not abandon you as orphans—
I will come to you.

John 14:18 NLT

A TIP FOR GUARDING YOUR HEART

Whenever you feel distant from God, that distance is your own doing, not His.

WORDS OF WISDOM

We need never shout across the spaces to an absent God. He is nearer than our own soul, closer than our most secret thoughts.

A. W. Tozer

There is nothing more important in any life than the constantly enjoyed presence of the Lord. There is nothing more vital, for without it we shall make mistakes, and without it we shall be defeated.

Alan Redpath

If your heart has grown cold, it is because you have moved away from the fire of His presence.

Beth Moore

Let this be your chief object in prayer: to realize the presence of your heavenly Father. Let your watchword be: Alone with God.

Andrew Murray

If you want to hear God's voice clearly and you are uncertain, then remain in His presence until He changes that uncertainty. Often, much can happen during this waiting for the Lord. Sometimes, he changes pride into humility, doubt into faith and peace.

Corrie ten Boom

GOD'S WORDS OF WISDOM

Again, this is God's command: to believe in his personally named Son, Jesus Christ. He told us to love each other, in line with the original command. As we keep his commands, we live deeply and surely in him, and he lives in us. And this is how we experience his deep and abiding presence in us: by the Spirit he gave us.

1 John 3:23-24 MSG

You will seek Me and find Me when you search for Me with all your heart.

Jeremiah 29:13 Holman CSB

For the eyes of the Lord range throughout the earth to strengthen those whose hearts are fully committed to him.

2 Chronicles 16:9 NIV

God did this so that men would seek him and perhaps reach out for him and find him, though he is not far from each one of us.

Acts 17:27 NIV

SUMMING IT UP

God is here, and He wants to establish an intimate relationship with you. When you sincerely reach out to Him, you will sense His presence.

GUARD YOUR STEPS
ONE DAY AT A TIME

Encourage one another daily, as long as it is Today . . . .

Hebrews 3:13 NIV

What do you expect from the day ahead? Are you expecting God to do wonderful things, or are you living beneath a cloud of apprehension and doubt? Do you expect God to use you in unexpected ways, or do you expect another uneventful day to pass with little fanfare? As a thoughtful believer, the answer to these questions should be obvious.

C. H. Spurgeon, the renowned 19th century English clergymen, advised, "Rejoicing is clearly a spiritual command. To ignore it, I need to remind you, is disobedience." As Christians, we are called by our Creator to live abundantly, prayerfully, and joyfully. To do otherwise is to squander His spiritual gifts.

Christ came to this earth to give us abundant life and eternal salvation. Our task is to accept Christ's grace with joy in our hearts and praise on our lips. When we fashion our days around Jesus, we are transformed: we see the world differently, we act differently, and we feel differently about ourselves and our neighbors.

If you're a thoughtful Christian, then you're a thankful Christian. And because of your faith, you can face the inevitable challenges and disappointments of each day armed with the joy of Christ and the promise of salvation.

So whatever this day holds for you, begin it and end it with God as your partner and Christ as your Savior. And throughout the day, give thanks to the One who created you and saved you. God's love for you is infinite—accept it joyfully and be thankful.

While it is daytime, we must continue
doing the work of the One who sent me.
Night is coming, when no one can work.

John 9:4 NCV

A TIP FOR GUARDING YOUR HEART

Take time to celebrate another day of life. And while you're at it, encourage your family and friends to join in the celebration.

WORDS OF WISDOM

As Christians, we must live a day at a time. No person, no matter how wealthy or gifted, can live two days at a time. God provides for us day by day.

Warren Wiersbe

He that fears not the future may enjoy the present.

Thomas Fuller

Let us live with urgency. Let us exploit the opportunity of life. Let us not drift. Let us live intentionally. We must not trifle our lives away.

Raymond Ortlund

Live today fully, expressing gratitude for all you have been, all you are right now, and all you are becoming.

Melodie Beattie

Submit each day to God, knowing that He is God over all your tomorrows.

Kay Arthur

GOD'S WORDS OF WISDOM

For he says, "In the time of my favor I heard you, and in the day of salvation I helped you." I tell you, now is the time of God's favor, now is the day of salvation.

2 Corinthians 6:2 NIV

Give your entire attention to what God is doing right now, and don't get worked up about what may or may not happen tomorrow. God will help you deal with whatever hard things come up when the time comes.

Matthew 6:34 MSG

This is the day which the LORD has made; let us rejoice and be glad in it.

Psalm 118:24 NASB

Therefore, get your minds ready for action, being self-disciplined, and set your hope completely on the grace to be brought to you at the revelation of Jesus Christ.

1 Peter 1:13 Holman CSB

SUMMING IT UP

Today is a wonderful, one-of-a-kind gift from God. Treat it that way.

GUARD YOUR STEPS BY WORKING DILIGENTLY

Work hard so God can approve you.
Be a good worker, one who does not need to be ashamed
and who correctly explains the word of truth

2 Timothy 2:15 NLT

Have you acquired the habit of doing first things first, or are you one of those people who put off important work until the last minute? The answer to this simple question will help determine how well you do your work and how much fun you have doing it.

God's Word teaches the value of hard work. In his second letter to the Thessalonians, Paul warns, " . . . if any would not work, neither should he eat" (3:10 KJV). And the Book of Proverbs proclaims, "One who is slack in his work is brother to one who destroys" (18:9 NIV). In short, God has created a world in which diligence is rewarded and laziness is not. So, whatever it is that you choose to do, do it with commitment, excitement, and vigor. And remember this: Hard work is not simply a proven way to get ahead; it's also part of God's plan for you.

Norman Vincent Peale said, "Think enthusiastically about everything, especially your work." If you're wise, you'll take that advice. When you do, you'll soon discover that the old saying is true: attitude determines altitude.

You have countless opportunities to accomplish great things for your God, for your family, and for yourself—but you should not expect the work to be easy. So pray as if everything depended upon God, but work as if everything depended upon you. When you do, you should expect very big payoffs. Why? Because when you and God become partners in your work, amazing things are bound to happen.

He did it with all his heart. So he prospered.

2 Chronicles 31:21 NKJV

A Tip for Guarding Your Heart

Here's a time-tested formula for success: have faith in God and do the work. It has been said that there are no shortcuts to any place worth going. Hard work is not simply a proven way to get ahead, it's also part of God's plan for all His children (including you).

WORDS OF WISDOM

Ordinary work, which is what most of us do most of the time, is ordained by God every bit as much as is the extraordinary.

Elisabeth Elliot

The world does not consider labor a blessing, therefore it flees and hates it, but the pious who fear the Lord labor with a ready and cheerful heart, for they know God's command, and they acknowledge His calling.

Martin Luther

If, in your working hours, you make the work your end, you will presently find yourself all unawares inside the only circle in your profession that really matters. You will be one of the sound craftsmen, and other sound craftsmen will know it.

C. S. Lewis

Few things fire up a person's commitment like dedication to excellence.

John Maxwell

Freedom is not an absence of responsibility; but rather a reward we receive when we've performed our responsibility with excellence.

Charles Swindoll

GOD'S WORDS OF WISDOM

In all the work you are doing, work the best you can. Work as if you were doing it for the Lord, not for people.

Colossians 3:23 NCV

Be strong and brave, and do the work. Don't be afraid or discouraged, because the Lord God, my God, is with you. He will not fail you or leave you."

1 Chronicles 28:20 NCV

But thanks be to God, who gives us the victory through our Lord Jesus Christ. Therefore, my beloved brethren, be steadfast, immovable, always abounding in the work of the Lord, knowing that your labor is not in vain in the Lord.

1 Corinthians 15:57-58 NKJV

Each of us will be rewarded for his own hard work.

1 Corinthians 3:8 TLB

SUMMING IT UP

When you find work that pleases God—and when you apply yourself conscientiously to the job at hand—you'll be rewarded.

GUARD YOUR STEPS BY WORSHIPPING GOD

Happy are those who hear the joyful call to worship,
for they will walk in the light of your presence, Lord.

Psalm 89:15 NLT

God's Word makes it clear: we should offer our Creator the praise and worship He deserves—and we shouldn't wait until Sunday morning to do so. Yet we live in a distraction-filled society that encourages us to make praise and worship a one-day-a-week activity.

If we allow the distractions of everyday living to interfere with the practice of regular worship and praise—or if we yield to the countless temptations of our world—we find ourselves engaged in a struggle between good and evil, a clash between God and Satan. Our responses to these struggles have implications that echo throughout our families and throughout our communities.

Some people may tell you that they don't engage in regular worship. Don't believe them. All of mankind is engaged in worship. The question is not whether we worship, but what we worship. Wise men and women choose to worship God. When they do, they are blessed with a plentiful harvest of joy, peace, and abundance. Other people choose to distance themselves from God by foolishly worshiping things that are intended to bring personal gratification, not spiritual gratification. Such choices often have tragic consequences.

Every day provides opportunities to put God where He belongs: at the center of your life. When you do so, you will worship Him with words, with prayers, and with deeds—and that's as it should be. For believers like you, God must come first. Always first.

Do you desire a life of abundance and peace? If so, find time to worship God every day of the week, not just on Sunday. He deserves no less . . . and neither, for that matter, do you.

If any man thirst, let him come unto me, and drink.
John 7:37 KJV

A TIP FOR GUARDING YOUR HEART

The best way to worship God . . . is to worship Him sincerely and often.

WORDS OF WISDOM

It's our privilege to not only raise our hands in worship but also to combine the visible with the invisible in a rising stream of praise and adoration sent directly to our Father.

Shirley Dobson

Our forgiveness of others becomes an act of worship that we would not enter into except for Who He is and for the overwhelming debt of love we owe Him.

Anne Graham Lotz

The fact that we were created to enjoy God and to worship him forever is etched upon our souls.

Jim Cymbala

Praise Him! Praise Him! Tell of His excellent greatness. Praise Him! Praise Him! Ever in joyful song!

Fanny Crosby

God asks that we worship Him with our concentrated minds as well as with our wills and emotions. A divided and scattered mind is not effective.

Catherine Marshall

GOD'S WORDS OF WISDOM

A time is coming and has now come when the true worshipers will worship the Father in spirit and truth, for they are the kind of worshipers the Father seeks. God is spirit, and his worshipers must worship in spirit and in truth.

John 4:23-24 NIV

For it is written, "You shall worship the Lord your God, and Him only you shall serve."

Matthew 4:10 NKJV

But seek first his kingdom and his righteousness, and all these things will be given to you as well.

Matthew 6:33 NIV

God lifted him high and honored him far beyond anyone or anything, ever, so that all created beings in heaven and earth, even those long ago dead and buried, will bow in worship before this Jesus Christ, and call out in praise that he is the Master of all, to the glorious honor of God the Father.

Philippians 2:9-11 MSG

SUMMING IT UP

When you worship God with a sincere heart, He will guide your steps.

Guard Your Steps by Leading a Disciplined Lifestyle

If the Lord delights in a man's way, he makes his steps firm.

Psalm 37:23 NIV

God's Word reminds us again and again that our Creator expects us to lead disciplined lives. God doesn't reward laziness, misbehavior, or apathy. To the contrary, He expects us to behave with dignity and discipline. But ours is a world in which dignity and discipline are often in short supply.

We live in a world in which leisure is glorified and indifference is often glamorized. But God has other plans. God gives us talents, and He expects us to use them. But it is not always easy to cultivate those talents. Sometimes, we must invest countless hours (or, in some cases, many years) honing our skills. And that's perfectly okay with God, because He understands that self-discipline is a blessing, not a burden.

Proverbs 23:12 advises: "Apply your heart to discipline And your ears to words of knowledge" (NASB). And, 2 Peter 1:5-6 teaches, "make every effort to supplement your faith with goodness, goodness with knowledge, knowledge with self-control, self-control with endurance, endurance with godliness" (Holman CSB). Thus, God's Word is clear: we must exercise self-discipline in all matters.

When we pause to consider how much work needs to be done, we realize that self-discipline is not simply a proven way to get ahead, it's also an integral part of God's plan for our lives. If we genuinely seek to be faithful stewards of our time, our talents, and our resources, we must adopt a disciplined approach to life. Otherwise, our talents are wasted and our resources are squandered.

Life's greatest rewards seldom fall into our laps; to the contrary, our greatest accomplishments usually require work, perseverance, and discipline. May we, as disciplined believers, be willing to work for the rewards we so earnestly desire.

A TIP FOR GUARDING YOUR HEART

Understand that a disciplined lifestyle gives you more control. The more disciplined you become, the more you can take control over your life (which, by the way, is far better than letting your life take control over you).

WORDS OF WISDOM

"They that sow bountifully shall reap also bountifully," is as true in spiritual things as in material.

Lottie Moon

Work is doing it. Discipline is doing it every day. Diligence is doing it well every day.

Dave Ramsey

Personal humility is a spiritual discipline and the hallmark of the service of Jesus.

Franklin Graham

As we make an offering of our work, we find the truth of a principle Jesus taught: Fulfillment is not a goal to achieve, but always the by-product of a sacrifice.

Elisabeth Elliot

Working in the vineyard, working all the day, never be discouraged, only watch and pray.

Fanny Crosby

GOD'S WORDS OF WISDOM

Do you not know that those who run in a race all run, but only one receives the prize? Run in such a way that you may win. Everyone who competes in the games exercises self-control in all things.

1 Corinthians 9:24-25 NASB

I discipline my body and bring it under strict control, so that after preaching to others, I myself will not be disqualified.

1 Corinthians 9:27 Holman CSB

So prepare your minds for service and have self-control.

1 Peter 1:13 NCV

So don't lose a minute in building on what you've been given, complementing your basic faith with good character, spiritual understanding, alert discipline, passionate patience, reverent wonder, warm friendliness, and generous love, each dimension fitting into and developing the others.

2 Peter 1:5-7 MSG

SUMMING IT UP

If you choose to lead a disciplined lifestyle, your steps will be protected. If you choose to lead an undisciplined lifestyle, your steps will be misdirected.

GUARD YOUR STEPS BY WALKING IN CHRIST'S FOOTSTEPS

*"Follow Me," Jesus told them, "and I will make you into
fishers of men!" Immediately they left their nets and followed Him.*

Mark 1:17-18 Holman CSB

When Jesus addressed His disciples, He warned that
each one must "take up his cross and follow me."
The disciples must have known exactly what the
Master meant. In Jesus' day, prisoners were forced to carry
their own crosses to the location where they would be put to
death. Thus, Christ's message was clear: in order to follow Him,
Christ's disciples must deny themselves and, instead, trust Him
completely. Nothing has changed since then.

If we are to be disciples of Christ, we must trust Him and
place Him at the very center of our beings. Jesus never comes
"next." He is always first. The paradox, of course, is that only by
sacrificing ourselves to Him do we gain salvation for ourselves.

The nineteenth-century writer Hannah Whitall Smith
observed, "The crucial question for each of us is this: What do
you think of Jesus, and do you yet have a personal acquaintance

with Him?" Indeed, the answer to that question will determine the quality, the course, and the direction of your life today and for all eternity.

Jesus has called upon believers of every generation (and that includes you) to walk with Him. Jesus promises that when you follow in His footsteps, He will teach you how to live freely and lightly (Matthew 11:28-30). And when Jesus makes a promise, you can depend upon it.

Are you worried or anxious? Be confident in the power of Christ. He will never desert you. Are you discouraged? Be courageous and call upon your Savior. He will protect you and use you according to His purposes. Do you seek to be a worthy disciple of the One from Galilee? Then pick up His cross today and every day of your life. When you do, He will bless you now . . . and forever.

If your life honors the name of Jesus,
he will honor you.

2 Thessalonians 1:12 MSG

A TIP FOR GUARDING YOUR HEART

Talk is cheap—real discipleship isn't. When it comes to being a disciple of Christ, make sure that you and your friends back up your words with deeds.

WORDS OF WISDOM

The word Christian is both a noun and an adjective. We need more adjective Christians, more Christian Christians, Christians who are more Christian in thought and spirit and deed as well as in name.

Vance Havner

There is no way that we can be effective disciples of Christ except through relentless pruning—the cutting away of non-fruitbearing suckers that sap our energies, but bear no fruit.

Selwyn Hughes

When Jesus put the little child in the midst of His disciples, He did not tell the little child to become like His disciples; He told the disciples to become like the little child.

Ruth Bell Graham

We cannot make disciples of others unless we are disciples ourselves.

Oswald Chambers

In our faith we follow in someone's steps. In our faith we leave footprints to guide others. It's the principle of discipleship.

Max Lucado

GOD'S WORDS OF WISDOM

Be imitators of God, therefore, as dearly loved children.

Ephesians 5:1 NIV

Work hard, but not just to please your masters when they are watching. As slaves of Christ, do the will of God with all your heart. Work with enthusiasm, as though you were working for the Lord rather than for people.

Ephesians 6:6-7 NLT

Then Jesus said to His disciples, "If anyone wants to come with Me, he must deny himself, take up his cross, and follow Me.

Matthew 16:24 Holman CSB

All of us who look forward to his Coming stay ready, with the glistening purity of Jesus' life as a model for our own.

1 John 3:3 MSG

SUMMING IT UP

Jesus has invited you to become His disciple. If you accept His invitation—and if you obey His commandments—you will be protected and blessed.

GUARD YOUR STEPS BY LIVING COURAGEOUSLY

Wait for the Lord; be courageous and let your heart be strong.
Wait for the Lord.

Psalm 27:14 Holman CSB

Every life (including yours) is an unfolding series of events: some fabulous, some not-so-fabulous, and some downright disheartening. When you reach the mountaintops of life, praising God is easy. But, when the storm clouds form overhead, your faith will be tested, sometimes to the breaking point. As a believer, you can take comfort in this fact: Wherever you find yourself, whether at the top of the mountain or the depths of the valley, God is there, and because He cares for you, you can live courageously.

Believing Christians have every reason to be courageous. After all, the ultimate battle has already been fought and won on the cross at Calvary. But, even dedicated followers of Christ may find their courage tested by the inevitable disappointments and tragedies that occur in the lives of believers and non-believers alike.

The next time you find your courage tested to the limit, guard your heart by remembering that God is as near as your next breath. And remember that He is your shield and your strength. Call upon Him in your hour of need and then be comforted. Whatever your challenge, whatever your trouble, God can handle it. And will.

Therefore, being always of good courage . . .
we walk by faith, not by sight.

2 Corinthians 5:6-7 NASB

A TIP FOR GUARDING YOUR HEART

With God as your partner, you have nothing to fear. Why? Because you and God, working together, can handle absolutely anything that comes your way. So the next time you'd like an extra measure of courage, recommit yourself to a true one-on-one relationship with Your Creator. When you sincerely turn to Him, He will never fail you.

WORDS OF WISDOM

Jesus Christ can make the weakest man into a divine dreadnought, fearing nothing.

Oswald Chambers

There comes a time when we simply have to face the challenges in our lives and stop backing down.

John Eldredge

Just as courage is faith in good, so discouragement is faith in evil, and, while courage opens the door to good, discouragement opens it to evil.

Hannah Whitall Smith

Perhaps I am stronger than I think.

Thomas Merton

God did away with all my fear. It was time for someone to stand up—or in my case, sit down. So I refused to move.

Rosa Parks

GOD'S WORDS OF WISDOM

Be strong and courageous, and do the work. Don't be afraid or discouraged by the size of the task, for the LORD God, my God, is with you. He will not fail you or forsake you.

1 *Chronicles 28:20 NLT*

God doesn't want us to be shy with his gifts, but bold and loving and sensible.

2 *Timothy 1:7 MSG*

The LORD himself goes before you and will be with you; he will never leave you nor forsake you. Do not be afraid; do not be discouraged.

Deuteronomy 31:8 NIV

But Moses said to the people, "Do not fear! Stand by and see the salvation of the LORD.

Exodus 14:13 NASB

SUMMING IT UP

If you are a disciple of the risen Christ, you have every reason on earth—and in heaven—to live courageously. And that's precisely what you should do.

GUARD YOUR STEPS BY OVERCOMING YOUR MISTAKES

Even though good people may be bothered by trouble seven times, they are never defeated.

Proverbs 24:16 NCV

When you experience failure, you must guard your heart. And make no mistake: you will experience failure. Life's occasional setbacks are simply the price that we all must pay for our willingness to take risks as we follow our dreams. But even when we encounter bitter disappointments, we must never lose faith.

Hebrews 10:36 advises, "Patient endurance is what you need now, so you will continue to do God's will. Then you will receive all that he has promised" (NLT). These words remind us that when we persevere, we will eventually receive the rewards which God has promised us. What's required is perseverance, not perfection.

When we face hardships, God stands ready to protect us. Our responsibility, of course, is to ask Him for protection. When we call upon Him in heartfelt prayer, He will answer—in His own time and according to His own plan—and He will do His part to heal us. We, of course, must do our part, too.

And, while we are waiting for God's plans to unfold and for His healing touch to restore us, we can be comforted in the knowledge that our Creator can overcome any obstacle, even if we cannot.

If you listen to constructive criticism,
you will be at home among the wise.

Proverbs 15:31 NLT

A TIP FOR GUARDING YOUR HEART

Failure isn't permanent . . . unless you fail to get up. So pick yourself up, dust yourself off, and trust God. He will make it right. Warren Wiersbe had this advice: "No matter how badly we have failed, we can always get up and begin again. Our God is the God of new beginnings." And don't forget: the best time to begin again is now.

WORDS OF WISDOM

As long as a man keeps his faith in God and in himself nothing can permanently defeat him.

Wilferd Peterson

Failure is one of life's most powerful teachers. How we handle our failures determines whether we're going to simply "get by" in life or "press on."

Beth Moore

God is able to take mistakes, when they are committed to Him, and make of them something for our good and for His glory.

Ruth Bell Graham

To have failed is to own more wisdom, understanding, and experience than do those who sit on life's sidelines playing it safe.

Susan Lenzkes

Success or failure can be pretty well predicted by the degree to which the heart is fully in it.

John Eldredge

GOD'S WORDS OF WISDOM

If we confess our sins to him, he is faithful and just to forgive us and to cleanse us from every wrong.

1 John 1:9 NLT

If you hide your sins, you will not succeed. If you confess and reject them, you will receive mercy.

Proverbs 28:13 NCV

So we're not giving up. How could we! Even though on the outside it often looks like things are falling apart on us, on the inside, where God is making new life, not a day goes by without his unfolding grace.

2 Corinthians 4:16 MSG

I waited patiently for the LORD; he turned to me and heard my cry. He lifted me out of the slimy pit, out of the mud and mire; he set my feet on a rock and gave me a firm place to stand. He put a new song in my mouth, a hymn of praise to our God . . . .

Psalm 40:1-3 NIV

SUMMING IT UP

Setbacks are inevitable—your response to them is optional. You can turn your stumbling blocks into stepping stones . . . and you should.

GUARD YOUR STEPS BY BEING GENEROUS

The generous soul will be made rich,
and he who waters will also be watered himself.

Proverbs 11:25 NKJV

When you give generously to those who need your help, God blesses your endeavors and enriches your life. So, if you're looking for a surefire way to improve the quality of your life, here it is: be more generous.

The thread of generosity is woven—completely and inextricably—into the very fabric of Christ's teachings. As He sent His disciples out to heal the sick and spread God's message of salvation, Jesus offered this guiding principle: Freely you have received, freely give. (Matthew 10:8 NIV) The principle still applies. If we are to be disciples of Christ, we must give freely of our time, our possessions, and our love.

In 2 Corinthians 9, Paul reminds us that when we sow the seeds of generosity, we reap bountiful rewards in accordance with God's plan for our lives. Thus, we are instructed to give cheerfully and without reservation: "But this I say: He who sows sparingly will also reap sparingly, and he who sows bountifully will also reap bountifully. So let each one give as he purposes in his heart, not grudgingly or of necessity; for God loves a cheerful giver." (v. 6-7 NKJV)

Today, you may feel the urge to hoard your blessings. Don't do it. Instead, give generously to those less fortunate than you, and do so without fanfare. Find a need and fill it . . . humbly. Lend a helping hand or share a word of kindness . . . anonymously. It's the godly thing to do—and it's the best way to live.

Be generous: Invest in acts of charity.
Charity yields high returns.

Ecclesiastes 11:1 MSG

A TIP FOR GUARDING YOUR HEART

Would you like to be a little happier? Try sharing a few more of the blessings that God has bestowed upon you. In other words, if you want to be happy, be generous. And if you want to be unhappy, be greedy.

WORDS OF WISDOM

He climbs highest who helps another up.

Zig Ziglar

Anything done for another is done for oneself.

Pope John Paul II

The mind grows by taking in, but the heart grows by giving out.

Warren Wiersbe

If there be any truer measure of a man than by what he does, it must be by what he gives.

Robert South

Let us give according to our incomes, lest God make our incomes match our gifts.

Peter Marshall

GOD'S WORDS OF WISDOM

God has given gifts to each of you from his great variety of spiritual gifts. Manage them well so that God's generosity can flow through you.

1 Peter 4:10 NLT

And above all these things put on charity, which is the bond of perfectness.

Colossians 3:14 KJV

In every way I've shown you that by laboring like this, it is necessary to help the weak and to keep in mind the words of the Lord Jesus, for He said, "It is more blessed to give than to receive."

Acts 20:35 Holman CSB

Whenever we have the opportunity, we should do good to everyone, especially to our Christian brothers and sisters.

Galatians 6:10 NLT

SUMMING IT UP

God has given so much to you, and He wants you to share His gifts with others.

GUARD YOUR STEPS BY MAKING GODLY CHOICES

If you need wisdom—if you want to know what
God wants you to do—ask him, and he will gladly tell you.
He will not resent your asking.

James 1:5 NLT

Life is a series of choices. From the instant we wake in the morning until the moment we nod off to sleep at night, we make countless decisions: decisions about the things we do, decisions about the words we speak, and decisions about the thoughts we choose to think. Simply put, the quality of those decisions determines the quality of our lives.

As believers who have been saved by a loving and merciful God, we have every reason to make wise choices. Yet sometimes, amid the inevitable hustle and bustle of life here on earth, we allow ourselves to behave in ways that we know are displeasing to our Creator. When we do, we forfeit the joy and the peace that we might otherwise experience through Him.

As you consider the next step in your life's journey, take time to consider how many things in this life you can control: your thoughts, your words, your priorities, and your actions, for starters. And then, if you sincerely want to discover God's purpose for your life, make choices that are pleasing to Him. He deserves no less . . . and neither do you.

Sometimes, because you're an imperfect human being, you may become so wrapped up in meeting society's expectations that you fail to focus on God's expectations. To do so is a mistake of major proportions—don't make it. Instead, seek God's guidance as you focus your energies on becoming the best "you" that you can possibly be. And, when it comes to matters of conscience, seek approval not from your peers, but from your Creator.

Whom will you try to please today: God or man? Your primary obligation is not to please imperfect men and women. Your obligation is to strive diligently to meet the expectations of an all-knowing and perfect God. Trust Him always. Love Him always. Praise Him always. And make choices that please Him. Always.

So I strive always to keep my conscience clear before God and man.

Acts 24:16 NIV

A TIP FOR GUARDING YOUR HEART

The quality of your choices will help determine the quality of your life. When you make better choices, you'll enjoy a better life.

WORDS OF WISDOM

Choices can change our lives profoundly. The choice to mend a broken relationship, to say "yes" to a difficult assignment, to lay aside some important work to play with a child, to visit some forgotten person—these small choices may affect many lives eternally.

Gloria Gaither

God expresses His love in giving us the freedom to choose.

Charles Stanley

Life is pretty much like a cafeteria line—it offers us many choices, both good and bad. The Christian must have a spiritual radar that detects the difference not only between bad and good but also among good, better, and best.

Dennis Swanberg

Faith is not a feeling; it is action. It is a willed choice.

Elisabeth Elliot

The choices of time are binding in eternity.

Jack MacArthur

GOD'S WORDS OF WISDOM

*I am offering you life or death, blessings or curses. Now, choose life!
. . . To choose life is to love the Lord your God, obey him, and stay
close to him.*

Deuteronomy 30:19-20 NCV

*The thing you should want most is God's kingdom and doing what
God wants. Then all these other things you need will be given to you.*

Matthew 6:33 NCV

*Now it happened as they went that He entered a certain village; and
a certain woman named Martha welcomed Him into her house. And
she had a sister called Mary, who also sat at Jesus' feet and heard
His word. But Martha was distracted with much serving, and she
approached Him and said, "Lord, do You not care that my sister
has left me to serve alone? Therefore tell her to help me." And Jesus
answered and said to her, "Martha, Martha, you are worried and
troubled about many things. But one thing is needed, and Mary has
chosen that good part, which will not be taken away from her."*

Luke 10:38-42 NKJV

SUMMING IT UP

Every step of your life's journey is a choice . . . and the quality
of those choices determines the quality of the journey.

GUARD YOUR STEPS BY LIVING ACCORDING TO YOUR BELIEFS

But prove yourselves doers of the word, and not merely hearers.
James 1:22 NASB

In describing our beliefs, our actions are far better descriptors than our words. Yet far too many of us spend more energy talking about our beliefs than living by them—with predictably poor results.

As believers, we must beware: Our actions should always give credence to the changes that Christ can make in the lives of those who walk with Him.

Your beliefs shape your values, and your values shape your life. Is your life a clearly-crafted picture book of your creed? Are your actions always consistent with your beliefs? Are you willing to practice the philosophies that you preach? Hopefully so; otherwise, you'll be tormented by inconsistencies between your beliefs and your behaviors.

If you want to guard your heart—and if you'd like to partake in the peace that only God can give—make certain that your actions are guided by His Word. And while you're at it, pay careful attention to the conscience that God, in His infinite wisdom, has placed in your heart. Don't treat your faith as if it were separate from your everyday life. Weave your beliefs into the very fabric of your day. When you do, God will honor your good works, and your good works will honor God.

If you seek to be a responsible believer, you must realize that it is never enough to hear the instructions of God; you must also live by them. And it is never enough to wait idly by while others to do God's work here on earth; you, too, must act. Doing God's work is a responsibility that every Christian (including you) should bear. And when you do, your loving Heavenly Father will reward your efforts with a bountiful harvest.

I know whom I have believed and am persuaded that He is able to guard what has been entrusted to me until that day.

2 Timothy 1:12 Holman CSB

A TIP FOR GUARDING YOUR HEART

You do not believe because you see and understand; you see and understand because you believe.

WORDS OF WISDOM

What I believe about God is the most important thing about me.

A. W. Tozer

I believe in Christ as I believe in that the Sun has risen, not only because I see it, but because by it I see everything else.

C. S. Lewis

The reason many of us do not ardently believe in the gospel is that we have never given it a rigorous testing, thrown our hard questions at it, or faced it with our most prickly doubts.

Eugene Peterson

I don't care what a man says he believes with his lips. I want to know with a vengeance what he says with his life and his actions.

Sam Jones

What we believe determines how we behave, and both determine what we become.

Warren Wiersbe

GOD'S WORDS OF WISDOM

Whoever believes that Jesus is the Christ is born of God, and everyone who loves Him who begot also loves him who is begotten of Him.

1 John 5:1 NKJV

You never saw him, yet you love him. You still don't see him, yet you trust him—with laughter and singing. Because you kept on believing, you'll get what you're looking forward to: total salvation.

1 Peter 1:8-9 MSG

Jesus summed it all up when he cried out, "Whoever believes in me, believes not just in me but in the One who sent me. Whoever looks at me is looking, in fact, at the One who sent me. I am Light that has come into the world so that all who believe in me won't have to stay any longer in the dark.

John 12:44-46 MSG

SUMMING IT UP

When you live in accordance with your beliefs, God will guide your steps and protect your heart.

GUARD YOUR STEPS BY TRUSTING GOD'S PLAN

*The Lord says, "I will guide you along the best pathway for your life.
I will advise you and watch over you."*

Psalm 32:8 NLT

Do you want to experience a life filled with abundance and peace? If so, here's a word of warning: you'll need to resist the temptation to do things "your way" and commit, instead, to do things God's way.

God has plans for your life. Big plans. But He won't force you to follow His will; to the contrary, He has given you free will, the ability to make decisions on your own. With the freedom to choose comes the responsibility of living with the consequences of the choices you make.

The most important decision of your life is, of course, your commitment to accept Jesus Christ as your personal Lord and Savior. And once your eternal destiny is secured, you will undoubtedly ask yourself the question "What now, Lord?" If you earnestly seek God's will for your life, you will find it . . . in time.

When you make the decision to seek God's will for your life, you will contemplate His Word, and you will be watchful for His signs. You will associate with fellow believers who will encourage your spiritual growth. And, you will listen to that inner voice that speaks to you in the quiet moments of your daily devotionals.

Sometimes, God's plans are crystal clear, but other times, He leads you through the wilderness before He delivers you to the Promised Land. So be patient, keep searching, and keep praying. If you do, then in time, God will answer your prayers and make His plans known.

God is right here, and He intends to use you in wonderful, unexpected ways. You'll discover those plans by doing things His way . . . and you'll be eternally grateful that you did.

Teach me Your way, O Lord;
I will walk in Your truth.

Psalm 86:11 NKJV

A TIP FOR GUARDING YOUR HEART

Big, bigger, and very big plans. God has very big plans in store for your life, so trust Him and wait patiently for those plans to unfold. And remember: God's timing is best.

WORDS OF WISDOM

It's incredible to realize that what we do each day has meaning in the big picture of God's plan.

Bill Hybels

God has a plan for the life of every Christian. Every circumstance, every turn of destiny, all things work together for your good and for His glory.

Billy Graham

When the dream of our heart is one that God has planted there, a strange happiness flows into us. At that moment, all of the spiritual resources of the universe are released to help us. Our praying is then at one with the will of God and becomes a channel for the Creator's purposes for us and our world.

Catherine Marshall

God prepared a plan for your life alone—and neither man nor the devil can destroy that plan.

Kay Arthur

God regularly and consistently takes all that He allows to happen to Christians, even what seems to them to be the worst things, and turns those events ultimately into blessings. That is divine providence at work.

John MacArthur

GOD'S WORDS OF WISDOM

And we know that in all things God works for the good of those who love him, who have been called according to his purpose.

Romans 8:28 NIV

The Lord shatters the plans of nations and thwarts all their schemes. But the Lord's plans stand firm forever; his intentions can never be shaken.

Psalm 33:10-11 NLT

Trust the Lord your God with all your heart and lean not on your own understanding; in all your ways acknowledge him, and he will make your paths straight.

Proverbs 3:5-6 NIV

There is one thing I always do. Forgetting the past and straining toward what is ahead, I keep trying to reach the goal and get the prize for which God called me . . . .

Philippians 3:13–14 NCV

SUMMING IT UP

God has a plan for your life. Your job is to discover that plan and follow it.

GUARD YOUR STEPS BY FOCUSING ON THE PRIZE

*Do you not know that the runners in a stadium all race,
but only one receives the prize? Run in such a way that you may win.
Now everyone who competes exercises self-control in everything.
However, they do it to receive a perishable crown,
but we an imperishable one.*

1 Corinthians 9:24-25 Holman CSB

A s you make your way through life, you will undoubtedly experience your fair share of disappointments, detours, false starts, and failures. Whenever you encounter one of life's dead ends, you're facing a test of character. And of course the question of the day is not if you'll be tested; it's how you will respond.

The old saying is as true today as it was when it was first spoken: "Life is a marathon, not a sprint." That's why wise travelers (like you) select a traveling companion who never tires and never falters. That partner, of course, is your Heavenly Father.

The next time you find your courage or your character tested to the limit, you must remember that God is as near as your next breath, and remember that He offers strength and comfort to His children. He is your shield and your strength; He is your protector and your deliverer. Call upon Him in your hour of need and then be comforted. Whatever your challenge, whatever your trouble, God can help you persevere. And that's precisely what He'll do if you ask Him.

Perhaps you are in a hurry for God to help you resolve your difficulties. Perhaps you're anxious to earn the rewards that you feel you've already earned from life. Perhaps you're drumming your fingers, impatiently waiting for God to act. If so, be forewarned: God operates on His own timetable, not yours. Sometimes, God may answer your prayers with silence, and when He does, you must patiently persevere. In times of trouble, you must remain steadfast and trust in the merciful goodness of your Heavenly Father. Whatever your problem, He can manage it. Your job is to keep persevering until He does.

It is better to finish something than to start it.
It is better to be patient than to be proud.

Ecclesiastes 7:8 NCV

A TIP FOR GUARDING YOUR HEART

If things don't work out at first, don't quit. If you never try, you'll never know how good you can be.

WORDS OF WISDOM

Are you a Christian? If you are, how can you be hopeless? Are you so depressed by the greatness of your problems that you have given up all hope? Instead of giving up, would you patiently endure? Would you focus on Christ until you are so preoccupied with him alone that you fall prostrate before him?

Anne Graham Lotz

Just remember, every flower that ever bloomed had to go through a whole lot of dirt to get there!

Barbara Johnson

Battles are won in the trenches, in the grit and grime of courageous determination; they are won day by day in the arena of life.

Charles Swindoll

The hardest part of a journey is neither the start nor the finish, but the middle mile.

Vance Havner

Untold damage has been done to the cause of Christ because some people gear up for a sprint when they need to train for the marathon.

Bill Hybels

GOD'S WORDS OF WISDOM

Patient endurance is what you need now, so you will continue to do God's will. Then you will receive all that he has promised.

Hebrews 10:36 NLT

Keep your eyes on Jesus, who both began and finished this race we're in. Study how he did it. Because he never lost sight of where he was headed—that exhilarating finish in and with God—he could put up with anything along the way: cross, shame, whatever. And now he's there, in the place of honor, right alongside God.

Hebrews 12:2 MSG

Thanks be to God! He gives us the victory through our Lord Jesus Christ. Therefore, my dear brothers, stand firm. Let nothing move you. Always give yourselves fully to the work of the Lord, because you know that your labor in the Lord is not in vain.

1 Corinthians 15:57-58 NIV

Be diligent that ye may be found of him in peace, without spot, and blameless.

2 Peter 3:14 KJV

SUMMING IT UP

Life is an exercise in perseverance. If you persevere, you win.

PART 4

GUARD
YOUR HEART

Jesus' Principles of Prayer

And when you pray, do not be like the hypocrites,
for they love to pray standing in the synagogues and on
the street corners to be seen by men. I tell you the truth,
they have received their reward in full. But when you pray,
go into your room, close the door and pray to your Father,
who is unseen. Then your Father, who sees what is done in secret,
will reward you. And when you pray, do not keep on
babbling like pagans, for they think they will be heard
because of their many words. Do not be like them,
for your Father knows what you need before you ask him.

Matthew 6:5-8 NIV

If you sincerely wish to guard your heart, no discipline is more important than the discipline of prayer. In the sixth chapter of Matthew, Jesus offers the Bible's first extensive instructions regarding prayer. It is here that Jesus offers five principles about prayer that still apply.

PRINCIPLE #1

Pray Regularly. Jesus began His lesson on prayer with the words, "And when you pray . . . " He did not say "if you pray." Prayer was assumed to be a regular daily activity for Christians. In truth, the Christian life cannot be maintained without consistent daily prayer.

Many Christians talk about their "prayer life." Yet God is not as interested in our having "prayer lives" as He is in our having "lives of prayer." And make no mistake: there's a big difference. A "prayer life" indicates that we divide our daily activities into times of prayer and times of non-prayer. What God prefers is that the entirety of a Christian's life should become a constant prayer lifted to Him—every activity dedicated to Him, every part of the day an act of worship.

PRINCIPLE #2

Pray Privately. Jesus teaches that our times of protracted, concentrated prayer are not to be public spectacles, but are to be private. He admonishes us to go into our rooms, to close the door, and to talk to our Father who is unseen.

Does this mean that we are to never pray publicly? No, but it does mean that most of our prayers are to be private communications, just between God and us.

Some folks may say, "Well, I pray with my family." And, of course, that's an admirable activity. Others may say, "I am in a prayer group at church." And once again, God will be pleased. But nothing should obscure the fact that the majority of our concentrated prayer times are to be private.

PRINCIPLE #3

Have a Time and Place for Prayer. What we schedule, we do. What we don't schedule, we may never get around to doing. So it's best to set aside a specific time for concentrated prayer.

Jesus had a set time of concentrated prayer—the early morning. Not a morning person? Then try the evening, or maybe during your lunch break. But whatever you do, have a regular, daily time of prayer . . . and have a place.

Jesus prayed outdoors; maybe you find that too distracting. If so, find a room where you can shut the door and pray. Do whatever works for you, but make certain that you have a specific place and time each day when you do nothing, absolutely nothing, but talk to the Father.

PRINCIPLE #4

Prayer Is Rewarded. We sometimes baulk at the idea that we will be rewarded for doing what we consider to be our duty. Yet if Jesus did not want us to know about the rewards of prayer, He would not have told us that "your Father, who sees what is done in secret, will reward you" (Matthew 6:6).

Do these rewards come now, or later? Of course, there may be many earthly rewards for prayer; and we most assuredly benefit from the blessings that arise from the act of praying. But we can also be certain that our prayers will be rewarded in heaven.

PRINCIPLE #5

Keep It Simple. Jesus said that we are not to pray, "babbling like pagans, for they think they will be heard because of their many words." He tells us that our Father knows what we need before we ask Him. So, we can keep our prayers short, sweet, and simple. We needn't try to impress God by fancy speeches or lengthy lectures. God isn't concerned with the eloquence of our words, which, by the way, is a very good thing. That means that all of us can talk intimately with God . . . and He always understands.

Rejoice always, pray without ceasing,
in everything give thanks;
for this is the will of God in Christ Jesus for you.
1 Thessalonians 5:16-18 NKJV

A TIP FOR GUARDING YOUR HEART

Even when prayer does not immediately change your circumstances, prayer changes you. So pray!

WORDS OF WISDOM

When you ask God to do something, don't ask timidly; put your whole heart into it.

Marie T. Freeman

God delights in the prayers of His children—prayers that express our love for Him, prayers that share our deepest burdens with Him.

Billy Graham

Are you weak? Weary? Confused? Troubled? Pressured? How is your relationship with God? Is it held in its place of priority? I believe the greater the pressure, the greater your need for time alone with Him.

Kay Arthur

The Christian on his knees sees more than the philosopher on tiptoe.

D. L. Moody

We must leave it to God to answer our prayers in His own wisest way. Sometimes, we are so impatient and think that God does not answer. God always answers! He never fails! Be still. Abide in Him.

Mrs. Charles E. Cowman

GOD'S WORDS OF WISDOM

If you don't know what you're doing, pray to the Father. He loves to help. You'll get his help, and won't be condescended to when you ask for it. Ask boldly, believingly, without a second thought. People who "worry their prayers" are like wind-whipped waves. Don't think you're going to get anything from the Master that way, adrift at sea, keeping all your options open.

James 1:5-8 MSG

The effective prayer of a righteous man can accomplish much.

James 5:16 NASB

Whatever you ask for in prayer, believe that you have received it, and it will be yours.

Mark 11:24 NIV

I sought the LORD, and he heard me, and delivered me from all my fears.

Psalm 34:4 KJV

SUMMING IT UP

Prayer changes things and it changes you. So pray.

GUARD YOUR HEART BY FEARING GOD

The fear of the Lord is the beginning of knowledge,
but fools despise wisdom and instruction.

Proverbs 1:7 NKJV

Do you possess a healthy, fearful respect for God's power? Hopefully so. After all, the lesson from the Book of Proverbs is clear: "The fear of the Lord is the beginning of knowledge, but fools despise wisdom and instruction" (1:7 NKJV). Yet, you live in a world that often ignores the role that God plays in shaping the affairs of mankind. You live in a world where too many people consider it "unfashionable" or "unseemly" to discuss the fear of God. Don't count yourself among their number.

To fear God is to acknowledge His sovereignty over every aspect of His creation (including you). To fear God is to place your relationship with God in its proper perspective (He is your master; you are His servant). To fear God is to dread the very thought of disobeying Him. To fear God is to humble yourself in the presence of His infinite power and His infinite love.

God praises humility and punishes pride. That's why God's greatest servants will always be those humble men and women who care less for their own glory and more for God's glory. In God's kingdom, the only way to achieve greatness is to shun it. And the only way to be wise is to understand these facts: God is great; He is all-knowing; and He is all-powerful. We must respect Him, and we must humbly obey His commandments, or we must accept the consequences of our misplaced pride.

When we fear the Creator—and when we honor Him by obeying His teachings—we receive God's approval and His blessings. But, when we ignore Him or disobey His commandments, we invite disastrous consequences.

God's hand shapes the universe, and it shapes our lives. God maintains absolute sovereignty over His creation, and His power is beyond comprehension. As believers, we must cultivate a sincere respect for God's awesome power. The fear of the Lord is, indeed, the beginning of knowledge. So today, as you face the realities of everyday life, remember this: until you acquire a healthy, respectful fear of God's power, your education is incomplete, and so is your faith.

A TIP FOR GUARDING YOUR HEART

It's the right kind of fear: Your respect for God should make you fearful of disobeying Him . . . very fearful.

WORDS OF WISDOM

The remarkable thing about fearing God is that when you fear God, you fear nothing else, whereas if you do not fear God, you fear everything else.

Oswald Chambers

If we do not tremble before God, the world's system seems wonderful to us and pleasantly consumes us.

James Montgomery Boice

A healthy fear of God will do much to deter us from sin.

Charles Swindoll

It is not possible that mortal men should be thoroughly conscious of the divine presence without being filled with awe.

C. H. Spurgeon

When true believers are awed by the greatness of God and by the privilege of becoming His children, then they become sincerely motivated, effective evangelists.

Bill Hybels

GOD'S WORDS OF WISDOM

Honor all people. Love the brotherhood. Fear God. Honor the king.

1 Peter 2:17 NKJV

Fear the LORD your God, serve him only and take your oaths in his name.

Deuteronomy 6:13 NIV

The fear of the Lord is a fountain of life . . . .

Proverbs 14:27 NIV

How blessed is everyone who fears the LORD, who walks in His ways.

Psalm 128:1 NASB

To turn from evil is understanding.

Job 28:28 Holman CSB

SUMMING IT UP

When you possess a healthy fear of God, He will guide your steps and guard your heart.

GUARD YOUR HEART WHEN THINGS GO WRONG

I'm just as happy with little as with much, with much as with little.
I've found the recipe for being happy whether full or hungry,
hands full or hand empty. Whatever I have, wherever I am,
I can make it through anything in the One who makes me who I am.

Philippians 4:12-13 MSG

When things go wrong, it's easy to become discouraged. But a far better strategy is this: Work to change the things you can, and trust God to handle the rest.

The American Theologian Reinhold Niebuhr composed a profoundly simple verse that came to be known as the Serenity Prayer: "God, grant me the serenity to accept the things I cannot change, the courage to change the things I can, and the wisdom to know the difference." Niebuhr's words are far easier to recite than they are to live by. Why? Because most of us want life to unfold in accordance with to our own wishes and timetables. But sometimes God has other plans.

Author Hannah Whitall Smith observed, "How changed our lives would be if we could only fly through the days on wings of surrender and trust!" These words remind us that even when we cannot understand the workings of God, we must trust Him and accept His will.

So if you've encountered unfortunate circumstances that are beyond your power to control, accept those circumstances . . . and trust God. When you do, you can be comforted in the knowledge that your Creator is both loving and wise, and that He understands His plans perfectly, even when you do not.

He is the Lord. Let him do what he thinks is best.

1 Samuel 3:18 NCV

A TIP FOR GUARDING YOUR HEART

Acceptance means learning to trust God more. Today, think of at least one aspect of your life that you've been reluctant to accept, and then prayerfully ask God to help you trust Him more by accepting the past.

WORDS OF WISDOM

The greatness of a man's power is the measure of his surrender.

William Booth

Have courage for the great sorrows of life and patience for the small ones; and when you have laboriously accomplished your daily task, go to sleep in peace. God is awake.

Victor Hugo

This is the precept by which I have lived: Prepare for the worst; expect the best; and take what comes.

Robert E. Speer

Tomorrow's job is fathered by today's acceptance. Acceptance of what, at least for the moment, you cannot alter.

Max Lucado

The key to contentment is to consider. Consider who you are and be satisfied with that. Consider what you have and be satisfied with that. Consider what God's doing and be satisfied with that.

Luci Swindoll

GOD'S WORDS OF WISDOM

Shall I not drink from the cup the Father has given me?

John 18:11 NLT

The Lord says, "Forget what happened before, and do not think about the past. Look at the new thing I am going to do. It is already happening. Don't you see it? I will make a road in the desert and rivers in the dry land."

Isaiah 43:18-19 NCV

He said, "I came naked from my mother's womb, and I will be stripped of everything when I die. The LORD gave me everything I had, and the LORD has taken it away. Praise the name of the LORD!"

Job 1:21 NLT

Give in to God, come to terms with him and everything will turn out just fine.

Job 22:21 MSG

SUMMING IT UP

Do your best, and trust God to do the rest.

GUARD YOUR HEART DURING DIFFICULT DAYS

*When you go through deep waters and great trouble, I will be with
you. When you go through the rivers of difficulty, you will not drown!
When you walk through the fire of oppression,
you will not be burned up; the flames will not consume you.
For I am the Lord, your God . . . .*

Isaiah 43:2-3 NLT

As life here on earth unfolds, all of us encounter
occasional disappointments and setbacks: Those
occasional visits from Old Man Trouble are simply a
fact of life, and none of us are exempt. When tough times arrive,
we may be forced to rearrange our plans and our priorities. But
even on our darkest days, we must remember that God's love
remains constant.

The fact that we encounter adversity is not nearly so
important as the way we choose to deal with it. When tough
times arrive, we have a clear choice: we can begin the difficult
work of tackling our troubles . . . or not. When we summon
the courage to look Old Man Trouble squarely in the eye, he

usually blinks. But, if we refuse to address our problems, even the smallest annoyances have a way of growing into king-sized catastrophes.

Psalm 145 promises, "The Lord is near to all who call on him, to all who call on him in truth. He fulfills the desires of those who fear him; he hears their cry and saves them." (v. 18-20 NIV). And the words of Jesus offer us comfort: "These things I have spoken to you, that in Me you may have peace. In the world you will have tribulation; but be of good cheer, I have overcome the world" (John 16:33 NKJV).

As believers, we know that God loves us and that He will protect us. In times of hardship, He will comfort us; in times of sorrow, He will dry our tears. When we are troubled, or weak, or sorrowful, God is always with us. We must build our lives on the rock that cannot be shaken: we must trust in God. And then, we must get on with the hard work of tackling our problems . . . because if we don't, who will? Or should?

A TIP FOR GUARDING YOUR HEART

Talk about it . . . If you're having tough times, don't hit the panic button and don't keep everything bottled up inside. Find a person you can really trust and talk things over. A second opinion (or, for that matter, a third, fourth, or fifth opinion) is usually helpful.

WORDS OF WISDOM

A weak faith is weakened by predicaments and catastrophes whereas a strong faith is strengthened by them.

Victor Frankl

When you feel that all is lost, sometimes the greatest gain is ready to be yours.

Thomas à Kempis

Let's thank God for allowing us to experience troubles that drive us closer to Him.

Shirley Dobson

God may be in the process of pruning something out of your life at this very moment. If this is the case, don't fight it. Instead, welcome it, for His pruning will make you more fruitful and bring greater glory to the Father.

Rick Yohn

Christianity helps us face the music even when we don't like the tune.

Phillips Brooks

GOD'S WORDS OF WISDOM

We also have joy with our troubles, because we know that these troubles produce patience. And patience produces character, and character produces hope.

Romans 5:3-4 NCV

Don't fret or worry, Instead of worrying, pray. Let petitions and praises shape your worries into prayers, letting God know your concerns. Before you know it, a sense of God's wholeness, everything coming together for good, will come and settle you down.

Philippians 4:6-7 MSG

The LORD also will be a stronghold for the oppressed, a stronghold in times of trouble.

Psalm 9:9 NASB

You pulled me from the brink of death, my feet from the cliff-edge of doom. Now I stroll at leisure with God in the sunlit fields of life.

Psalm 56:13 MSG

SUMMING IT UP

When times are tough, you should guard your heart by turning it over to God.

GUARD YOUR HEART BY DIRECTING YOUR THOUGHTS

*Those who are pure in their thinking are happy,
because they will be with God.*

Matthew 5:8 NCV

How will you direct your thoughts today? Will you be an upbeat believer? Will you be a person whose hopes and dreams are alive and well? Will you put a smile on your face and a song in your heart? Hopefully so. But here's a word of warning: sometimes, when pessimism, anger, or doubt threaten to hijack your emotions, you won't feel much like celebrating. That's why you must always strive to keep your thoughts headed in the right direction.

Your thoughts have the power to lift you up or to drag you down; they have the power to energize you or deplete you, to inspire you to greater accomplishments or to make those accomplishments impossible.

What kind of attitude will you select today? Will you guard your heart by dwelling upon those things that are true, honorable, and worthy of praise? Or will you allow yourself to be swayed by the negativity that seems to dominate our troubled world?

God intends that you experience joy and abundance, but He will not force His joy upon you; you must claim it for yourself. It's up to you to celebrate the life that God has given you. So today, spend more time thinking about your blessings and less time fretting about your hardships. Then, take time to thank the Giver of all things good for gifts that are, in truth, far too numerous to count.

*So prepare your minds for service
and have self-control.*

1 Peter 1:13 NCV

A TIP FOR GUARDING YOUR HEART

Good thoughts can lead you to some very good places . . . and bad thoughts can lead elsewhere. So guard your thoughts accordingly.

WORDS OF WISDOM

God's cure for evil thinking is to fill our minds with that which is good.

George Sweeting

It is only by thinking about great and good things that we come to love them, and it is only by loving them that we come to long for them, and it is only by longing for them that we are impelled to seek after them; and it is only by seeking after them that they become ours.

Henry Van Dyke

I am amazed at my own "rut-think" that periodically takes over.

Marilyn Meberg

I became aware of one very important concept I had missed before: my attitude—not my circumstances—was what was making me unhappy.

Vonette Bright

It is the thoughts and intents of the heart that shape a person's life.

John Eldredge

GOD'S WORDS OF WISDOM

Come near to God, and God will come near to you. You sinners, clean sin out of your lives. You who are trying to follow God and the world at the same time, make your thinking pure.

James 4:8 NCV

And now, dear brothers and sisters, let me say one more thing as I close this letter. Fix your thoughts on what is true and honorable and right. Think about things that are pure and lovely and admirable. Think about things that are excellent and worthy of praise.

Philippians 4:8 NLT

Dear friend, guard Clear Thinking and Common Sense with your life; don't for a minute lose sight of them. They'll keep your soul alive and well, they'll keep you fit and attractive.

Proverbs 3:21-22 MSG

If your sinful nature controls your mind, there is death. But if the Holy Spirit controls your mind, there is life and peace.

Romans 8:6 NLT

SUMMING IT UP

Unless you're willing to guard your thoughts, you'll never be able to guard your heart.

GUARD YOUR HEART
WITH LOVE

And now abide faith, hope, love, these three;
but the greatest of these is love.

1 Corinthians 13:13 NKJV

L ove is a choice. Either you choose to behave lovingly toward others . . . or not; either you behave yourself in ways that enhance your relationships . . . or not. But make no mistake: genuine love requires effort. Simply put, if you wish to build lasting relationships, you must be willing to do your part.

Since the days of Adam and Eve, God has allowed His children to make choices for themselves, and so it is with you. As you interact with family and friends, you have choices to make . . . lots of them. If you choose wisely, you'll be rewarded; if you choose unwisely, you'll bear the consequences.

Christ's words are clear: we are to love God first, and secondly, we are to love others as we love ourselves (Matthew 22:37-40). These two commands are seldom easy, and because we are imperfect beings, we often fall short. But God's Holy Word commands us to try.

The Christian path is an exercise in love and forgiveness. If we are to walk in Christ's footsteps, we must forgive those who have done us harm, and we must accept Christ's love by sharing it freely with family, friends, neighbors, and even strangers.

God does not intend for you to experience mediocre relationships; He created you for far greater things. Building lasting relationships requires compassion, wisdom, empathy, kindness, courtesy, and forgiveness. If that sounds a lot like work, it is—which is perfectly fine with God. Why? Because He knows that you are capable of doing that work, and because He knows that the fruits of your labors will enrich the lives of your loved ones and the lives of generations yet unborn.

Love is the seed of all hope.
It is the enticement to trust, to risk,
to try, and to go on.

Gloria Gaither

A TIP FOR GUARDING YOUR HEART

Do you want love to last? Then you must understand this: Genuine love requires effort. That's why those who are lazy in love are often losers in love, too!

WORDS OF WISDOM

Love is an attribute of God. To love others is evidence of a genuine faith.

Kay Arthur

How do you spell love? When you reach the point where the happiness, security, and development of another person is as much of a driving force to you as your own happiness, security, and development, then you have a mature love. True love is spelled G-I-V-E. It is not based on what you can get, but rooted in what you can give to the other person.

Josh McDowell

Love must be supported and fed and protected, just like a little infant who is growing up at home.

James Dobson

It is when we come to the Lord in our nothingness, our powerlessness and our helplessness that He then enables us to love in a way which, without Him, would be absolutely impossible.

Elisabeth Elliot

GOD'S WORDS OF WISDOM

Though I speak with the tongues of men and of angels, but have not love, I have become sounding brass or a clanging cymbal.

1 Corinthians 13:1 NKJV

Beloved, if God so loved us, we also ought to love one another.

1 John 4:11 NASB

Love one another deeply, from the heart.

1 Peter 1:22 NIV

Above all, love each other deeply, because love covers over a multitude of sins.

1 Peter 4:8 NIV

May the Lord cause you to increase and abound in love for one another, and for all people.

1 Thessalonians 3:12 NASB

SUMMING IT UP

God is love, and He expects you to share His love with others.

GUARD YOUR HEART BY GROWING SPIRITUALLY

*Therefore, leaving the elementary message about the Messiah,
let us go on to maturity.*

Hebrews 6:1 Holman CSB

When it comes to your faith, God doesn't intend for you to stand still. He wants you to keep moving and growing. In fact, God's plan for you includes a lifetime of prayer, praise, and spiritual growth.

When we cease to grow, either emotionally or spiritually, we do ourselves and our loved ones a profound disservice. But, if we study God's Word, if we obey His commandments, and if we live in the center of His will, we will not be "stagnant" believers; we will, instead, be growing Christians . . . and that's exactly what God wants for our lives.

Many of life's most important lessons are painful to learn. During times of heartbreak and hardship, we must be courageous and we must be patient, knowing that in His own time, God will heal us if we invite Him into our hearts.

Spiritual growth need not take place only in times of adversity. We must seek to grow in our knowledge and love of the Lord every day that we live. In those quiet moments when we open our hearts to God, the One who made us keeps remaking us. He gives us direction, perspective, wisdom, and courage. The appropriate moment to accept those spiritual gifts is the present one.

When it comes to your faith, God doesn't intend for you to become "fully grown," at least not in this lifetime. In fact, God still has important lessons that He intends to teach you. So ask yourself this: what lesson is God trying to teach me today? And then go about the business of learning it.

Let the wise listen and add to their learning,
and let the discerning get guidance.

Proverbs 1:5 NIV

A TIP FOR GUARDING YOUR HEART

Spiritual maturity is a journey, not a destination. And the sooner you begin that journey, the farther you're likely to go.

WORDS OF WISDOM

You are either becoming more like Christ every day or you're becoming less like Him. There is no neutral position in the Lord.

Stormie Omartian

There is nothing more important than understanding God's truth and being changed by it, so why are we so casual about accepting the popular theology of the moment without checking it our for ourselves? God has given us a mind so that we can learn and grow. As his people, we have a great responsibility and wonderful privilege of growing in our understanding of him.

Sheila Walsh

How can God direct our steps if we're not taking any?

Sarah Leah Grafstein

We often become mentally and spiritually barren because we're so busy.

Franklin Graham

Don't go through life, grow through life.

Eric Butterworth

GOD'S WORDS OF WISDOM

Don't become so well-adjusted to your culture that you fit into it without even thinking. Instead, fix your attention on God. You'll be changed from the inside out. Readily recognize what he wants from you, and quickly respond to it. Unlike the culture around you, always dragging you down to its level of immaturity, God brings the best out of you, develops well-formed maturity in you.

Romans 12:2 MSG

He who began a good work in you will carry it on to completion until the day of Christ Jesus.

Philippians 1:6 NIV

Take my yoke upon you and learn from me . . . .

Matthew 11:29 NIV

But endurance must do its complete work, so that you may be mature and complete, lacking nothing.

James 1:4 Holman CSB

SUMMING IT UP

One way to guard your heart is by continuing to grow in your faith.

GUARD YOUR HEART BY PUTTING GOD FIRST

You shall have no other gods before Me.

Exodus 20:3 NKJV

One of the surest ways to guard your heart—perhaps the only way—is to do it with God as your partner. So here's a question worth thinking about: Have you made God your top priority by offering Him your heart, your soul, your talents, and your time? Or are you in the habit of giving God little more than a few hours on Sunday morning? The answer to these questions will determine, to a surprising extent, the direction of your day and the condition of your character.

As you contemplate your own relationship with God, remember this: all of mankind is engaged in the practice of worship. Some folks choose to worship God and, as a result, reap the joy that He intends for His children to experience. Other folks, folks who are stubbornly determined to do it "their way," distance themselves from God by worshiping such things as earthly possessions or personal gratification. . . . and when they do, they suffer.

In the book of Exodus, God warns that we should place no gods before Him (v. 20:3). Yet all too often, we place our Lord in second, third, or fourth place as we worship the gods of pride, greed, power, or lust.

Does God rule your heart? Make certain that the honest answer to this question is a resounding yes. If you sincerely wish to build your character and your life on an unshakable foundation, you must put your Creator in first place. No exceptions.

God is Spirit, and those who worship Him
must worship in spirit and truth.

John 4:24 Holman CSB

A Tip for Guarding Your Heart

Think about your priorities. Are you really putting God first in your life, or are you putting other things—things like possessions, pleasures, or personal status—ahead of your relationship with the Father. And if your priorities for life are misaligned, think of at least three things you can do today to put God where He belongs: in first place.

WORDS OF WISDOM

The man who is poor in spirit is the man who has realized that things mean nothing, and that God means everything.

William Barclay

Nature is too thin a screen; the glory of the omnipresent God bursts through everywhere.

Ralph Waldo Emerson

The infinity of God is not mysterious, it is only unfathomable— not concealed, but incomprehensible. It is a clear infinity—the darkness of the pure, unsearchable sea.

John Ruskin

A sense of deity is inscribed on every heart.

John Calvin

When all else is gone, God is still left. Nothing changes Him.

Hannah Whitall Smith

GOD'S WORDS OF WISDOM

Be still, and know that I am God . . . .

Psalm 46:10 KJV

For the Lord your God is the God of gods and Lord of lords, the great, mighty, and awesome God.

Deuteronomy 10:17 Holman CSB

The fool says in his heart, "God does not exist."

Psalm 14:1 Holman CSB

No one has seen God, ever. But if we love one another, God dwells deeply within us, and his love becomes complete in us—perfect love! This is how we know we're living steadily and deeply in him, and he in us: He's given us life from his life, from his very own Spirit.

1 John 4:12-13 MSG

God is love, and the one who remains in love remains in God, and God remains in him.

1 John 4:16 Holman CSB

SUMMING IT UP

You must guard your heart by putting God in His rightful place—first place.

Guard Your Heart with Bible Study

*All Scripture is inspired by God and is profitable for teaching,
for rebuking, for correcting, for training in righteousness,
so that the man of God may be complete,
equipped for every good work.*

2 Timothy 3:16-17 Holman CSB

God's Word will guard your heart if you read it every day. The Bible is a roadmap for life here on earth and for life eternal. As Christians, we are called upon to trust its promises, to follow its commandments, and to share its Good News.

As believers, we must study the Bible each day and meditate upon its meaning for our lives. Otherwise, we deprive ourselves of a priceless gift from our Creator. God's Holy Word is, indeed, a transforming, life-changing, one-of-a-kind treasure. And, a passing acquaintance with the Good Book is insufficient for Christians who seek to obey God's Word and to understand His will.

God has made promises to mankind and to you. God's promises never fail and they never grow old. You must trust those promises and share them with your family, with your friends, and with the world.

Are you standing on the promises of God? Are you expecting God to do wonderful things, or are you living beneath a cloud of apprehension and doubt? The familiar words of Psalm 118:24 remind us of a profound yet simple truth: "This is the day which the Lord hath made; we will rejoice and be glad in it" (KJV). Do you trust that promise, and do you live accordingly? If so, you are living the passionate life that God intends.

For passionate believers, every day begins and ends with God's Son and God's promises. When we accept Christ into our hearts, God promises us the opportunity for earthy peace and spiritual abundance. But more importantly, God promises us the priceless gift of eternal life.

As we face the inevitable challenges of life-here-on-earth, we must arm ourselves with the promises of God's Holy Word. When we do, we can expect the best, not only for the day ahead, but also for all eternity.

Your word is a lamp to my feet and a light for my path.

Psalm 119:105 NIV

A Tip for Guarding Your Heart

"Head knowledge" is important, but "heart knowledge" is imperative.

WORDS OF WISDOM

God's Word is not merely letters on paper . . . it's alive. Believe and draw near, for it longs to dance in your heart and whisper to you in the night.

Lisa Bevere

God can see clearly no matter how dark or foggy the night is. Trust His Word to guide you safely home.

Lisa Whelchel

Words fail to express my love for this holy Book, my gratitude for its author, for His love and goodness. How shall I thank him for it?

Lottie Moon

Never water down the word of God; preach it in its undiluted sternness.

Oswald Chambers

A thorough knowledge of the Bible is worth more than a college education.

Theodore Roosevelt

GOD'S WORDS OF WISDOM

So then faith comes by hearing, and hearing by the word of God.

Romans 10:17 NKJV

The words of the Lord are pure words, like silver tried in a furnace . . . .

Psalm 12:6 NKJV

Blessed are those who hunger and thirst for righteousness, For they shall be filled.

Matthew 5:6 NKJV

Jesus answered, "It is written: 'Man does not live by bread alone, but on every word that comes from the mouth of God.'"

Matthew 4:4 NIV

SUMMING IT UP

God's Word can guide your steps and guard your heart. Let your Bible be your guide.

GUARD YOUR HEART WITH MOUNTAIN-MOVING FAITH

*For truly I say to you, if you have faith as a mustard seed,
you shall say to this mountain, "Move from here to there"
and it shall move; and nothing shall be impossible to you.*

Matthew 17:20 NASB

B ecause we live in a demanding world, all of us have mountains to climb and mountains to move. Moving those mountains requires faith.

Are you a mountain mover whose faith is evident for all to see? Or, are you a spiritual shrinking violet? God needs more men and women who are willing to move mountains for His glory and for His kingdom.

Jesus taught His disciples that if they had faith, they could move mountains. You can too. When you place your faith, your trust, indeed your life in the hands of Christ Jesus, you'll be amazed at the marvelous things He can do. So strengthen your faith through praise, through worship, through Bible study, and through prayer. And trust God's plans. With Him, all things are possible, and He stands ready to open a world of possibilities to you . . . if you have faith.

Concentration camp survivor Corrie ten Boom relied on faith during her long months of imprisonment and torture. Later, despite the fact that four of her family members had died in Nazi death camps, Corrie's faith was unshaken. She wrote, "There is no pit so deep that God's love is not deeper still." Christians take note: Genuine faith in God means faith in all circumstances, happy or sad, joyful or tragic.

If your faith is being tested to the point of breaking, remember that Your Savior is near. If you reach out to Him in faith, He will give you peace and strength. Reach out today. If you touch even the smallest fragment of the Master's garment, He will make you whole. And then, with no further ado, let the mountain moving begin.

Be on the alert, stand firm in the faith,
act like men, be strong.

1 Corinthians 16:13 NASB

A TIP FOR GUARDING YOUR HEART

Base your faith on a decision to trust God, not on the emotions that you may be feeling at a particular moment.

WORDS OF WISDOM

There are a lot of things in life that are difficult to understand. Faith allows the soul to go beyond what the eyes can see.

John Maxwell

The popular idea of faith is of a certain obstinate optimism: the hope, tenaciously held in the face of trouble, that the universe is fundamentally friendly and things may get better.

J. I. Packer

I am truly grateful that faith enables me to move past the question of "Why?"

Zig Ziglar

Joy is faith feasting and celebrating the One in Whom it trusts.

Susan Lenzkes

Just as our faith strengthens our prayer life, so do our prayers deepen our faith. Let us pray often, starting today, for a deeper, more powerful faith.

Shirley Dobson

GOD'S WORDS OF WISDOM

For whatever is born of God overcomes the world. And this is the victory that has overcome the world—our faith.

1 John 5:4 NKJV

Fight the good fight of faith; take hold of the eternal life to which you were called . . . .

1 Timothy 6:12 NASB

Therefore, being always of good courage . . . we walk by faith, not by sight.

2 Corinthians 5:6-7 NASB

I have fought the good fight, I have finished the race, I have kept the faith.

2 Timothy 4:7 NIV

SUMMING IT UP

If your faith is strong enough, you and God—working together—can move mountains.

GUARD YOUR HEART AGAINST WORLDLINESS

You know the next commandment pretty well, too:
"Don't go to bed with another's spouse." But don't think you've
preserved your virtue simply by staying out of bed. Your heart can be
corrupted by lust even quicker than your body.
Those leering looks you think nobody notices—they also corrupt.

Matthew 5:27-28 MSG

We live in the world, but we should not worship it—yet at every turn, or so it seems, we are tempted to do otherwise. As Warren Wiersbe correctly observed, "Because the world is deceptive, it is dangerous."

The 21st Century world in which we live is a noisy, distracting place, a place that offers countless temptations and dangers. The world seems to cry, "Worship me with your time, your money, your energy, your thoughts, and your life!" But if we are wise, we won't fall prey to that temptation.

If you wish to build your character day-by-day, you must distance yourself, at least in part, from the temptations and distractions of modern-day society. But distancing yourself isn't easy, especially when so many societal forces are struggling to capture your attention, your participation, and your money.

C. S. Lewis said, "Aim at heaven and you will get earth thrown in; aim at earth and you will get neither." That's good advice. You're likely to hit what you aim at, so aim high . . . aim at heaven. When you do, you'll be strengthening your character as you improve every aspect of your life. And God will demonstrate His approval as He showers you with more spiritual blessings than you can count.

For whatever is born of God overcomes the world. And this is the victory that has overcome the world— our faith.

1 John 5:4 NKJV

A TIP FOR GUARDING YOUR HEART

Remember: if you seek the things that God values, you will be satisfied; if you seek the things that the world values, you will be disappointed.

WORDS OF WISDOM

The more we stuff ourselves with material pleasures, the less we seem to appreciate life.

Barbara Johnson

The Lord Jesus Christ is still praying for us. He wants us to be in the world but not of it.

Charles Stanley

The only ultimate disaster that can befall us, I have come to realize, is to feel ourselves to be home on earth.

Max Lucado

The true Christian, though he is in revolt against the world's efforts to brainwash him, is no mere rebel for rebellion's sake. He dissents from the world because he knows that it cannot make good on its promises.

A. W. Tozer

All those who look to draw their satisfaction from the wells of the world—pleasure, popularity, position, possessions, politics, power, prestige, finances, family, friends, fame, fortune, career, children, church, clubs, sports, sex, success, recognition, reputation, religion, education, entertainment, exercise, honors, health, hobbies—will soon be thirsty again!

Anne Graham Lotz

GOD'S WORDS OF WISDOM

Do not love the world or the things in the world. If you love the world, the love of the Father is not in you.

1 John 2:15 NCV

Let no one deceive himself. If anyone among you seems to be wise in this age, let him become a fool that he may become wise. For the wisdom of this world is foolishness with God. For it is written, "He catches the wise in their own craftiness."

1 Corinthians 3:18–19 NKJV

Religion that God our Father accepts as pure and faultless is this: to look after orphans and widows in their distress and to keep oneself from being polluted by the world.

James 1:27 NIV

If you lived on the world's terms, the world would love you as one of its own. But since I picked you to live on God's terms and no longer on the world's terms, the world is going to hate you.

John 15:19 MSG

SUMMING IT UP

Your world is full of distractions and temptations. Your challenge is to live in the world but not be of the world.

GUARD YOUR HEART WITH A POSITIVE ATTITUDE

And now, dear brothers and sisters, let me say one more thing
as I close this letter. Fix your thoughts on what is true and honorable
and right. Think about things that are pure and lovely and admirable.
Think about things that are excellent and worthy of praise.

Philippians 4:8 NLT

The Christian life is a cause for celebration, but sometimes we don't feel much like celebrating. In fact, when the weight of the world seems to bear down upon our shoulders, celebration may be the last thing on our minds . . . but it shouldn't be. As God's children, we are all blessed beyond measure on good days and bad. This day is a non-renewable resource—once it's gone, it's gone forever. We should give thanks for this day while using it for the glory of God.

What's your attitude today? Are you fearful, angry, bored, or worried? Are you pessimistic, perplexed, pained, and perturbed? Are you moping around with a frown on your face that's almost as big as the one in your heart? If so, God wants to have a little talk with you.

God created you in His own image, and He wants you to experience joy, contentment, peace, and abundance. But, God will not force you to experience these things; you must claim them for yourself.

God has given you free will, including the ability to influence the direction and the tone of your thoughts. And, here's how God wants you to direct those thoughts:

"Finally brothers, whatever is true, whatever is honorable, whatever is just, whatever is pure, whatever is lovely, whatever is commendable—if there is any moral excellence and if there is any praise—dwell on these things" (Philippians 4:8 Holman CSB).

The quality of your attitude will help determine the quality of your life, so you must guard your thoughts accordingly. If you make up your mind to approach life with a healthy mixture of realism and optimism, you'll be rewarded. But, if you allow yourself to fall into the unfortunate habit of negative thinking, you will doom yourself to unhappiness, or mediocrity, or worse.

So, the next time you find yourself dwelling upon the negative aspects of your life, refocus your attention on things positive. The next time you find yourself falling prey to the blight of pessimism, stop yourself and turn your thoughts around. The next time you're tempted to waste valuable time gossiping or complaining, resist those temptations with all your might. And remember: You'll never whine your way to the top . . . so don't waste your breath.

A TIP FOR GUARDING YOUR HEART

Attitudes are contagious, so it's important to associate with people who are upbeat, optimistic, and encouraging.

WORDS OF WISDOM

Life is 10% what happens to you and 90% how you respond to it.

Charles Swindoll

No matter how little we can change about our circumstances, we always have a choice about our attitude toward the situation.

Vonette Bright

All things being equal, attitude wins. All things not being equal, attitude sometimes still wins.

John Maxwell

The difference between winning and losing is how we choose to react to disappointment.

Barbara Johnson

I have witnessed many attitudes make a positive turnaround through prayer.

John Maxwell

GOD'S WORDS OF WISDOM

There is one thing I always do. Forgetting the past and straining toward what is ahead, I keep trying to reach the goal and get the prize for which God called me . . . .

Philippians 3:13–14 NCV

For God has not given us a spirit of fear, but of power and of love and of a sound mind.

2 Timothy 1:7 NLT

Keep your eyes focused on what is right, and look straight ahead to what is good.

Proverbs 4:25 NCV

You were taught, with regard to your former way of life, to put off your old self, which is being corrupted by its deceitful desires; to be made new in the attitude of your minds; and to put on the new self, created to be like God in true righteousness and holiness.

Ephesians 4:22-24 NIV

SUMMING IT UP

A positive attitude leads to positive results; a negative attitude leads elsewhere.

GUARD YOUR HEART AGAINST WORRY

Don't worry about anything, but in everything,
through prayer and petition with thanksgiving,
let your requests be made known to God.

Philippians 4:6 Holman CSB

Because we are imperfect human beings struggling with imperfect circumstances, we worry. Even though we, as Christians, have the assurance of salvation—even though we, as Christians, have the promise of God's love and protection—we find ourselves fretting over the inevitable frustrations of everyday life. Jesus understood our concerns when He spoke the reassuring words found in the 6th chapter of Matthew.

Where is the best place to take your worries? Take them to God. Take your troubles to Him; take your fears to Him; take your doubts to Him; take your weaknesses to Him; take your sorrows to Him . . . and leave them all there. Seek protection from the One who offers you eternal salvation; build your spiritual house upon the Rock that cannot be moved.

Perhaps you are concerned about your future, your health, or your finances. Or perhaps you are simply a "worrier" by nature.

If so, make Matthew 6 a regular part of your daily Bible reading. This beautiful passage will remind you that God still sits in His heaven and you are His beloved child. Then, perhaps, you will worry a little less and trust God a little more, and that's as it should be because God is trustworthy . . . and you are protected.

Yea, though I walk through the valley
of the shadow of death, I will fear no evil:
for thou art with me;
thy rod and thy staff they comfort me.

Psalm 23:4 KJV

A TIP FOR GUARDING YOUR HEART

An important part of becoming a more mature Christian is learning to worry less and to trust God more. And while you're at it, remember that worry is never a valid substitute for work. So do your best, and then turn your worries over to God.

WORDS OF WISDOM

For each of us, the time is surely coming when we shall have nothing but God. Health and wealth and friends and hiding places will all be swept away, and we shall have only God. To the man of pseudo faith this is a terrifying thought, but to a man of real faith, it is one of the most comforting thoughts the heart can entertain.

A. W. Tozer

Faith is nothing more or less than actively trusting God.

Catherine Marshall

As God's children, we are the recipients of lavish love—a love that motivates us to keep trusting even when we have no idea what God is doing.

Beth Moore

Never imagine that you can be a loser by trusting in God.

C. H. Spurgeon

We trust not because "a God" exists, but because this God exists.

C. S. Lewis

GOD'S WORDS OF WISDOM

So do not worry, saying, "What shall we eat?" or "What shall we drink?" or "What shall we wear?" For the pagans run after all these things, and your heavenly Father knows that you need them. But seek first his kingdom and his righteousness, and all these things will be given to you as well. Therefore do not worry about tomorrow, for tomorrow will worry about itself. Each day has enough trouble of its own.

Matthew 6:31-34 NIV

Come to Me, all you who labor and are heavy laden, and I will give you rest. Take My yoke upon you and learn from Me, for I am gentle and lowly in heart, and you will find rest for your souls. For My yoke is easy and My burden is light.

Matthew 11:28-30 NKJV

I was very worried, but you comforted me . . . .

Psalm 94:19 NCV

An anxious heart weighs a man down . . . .

Proverbs 12:25 NIV

SUMMING IT UP

Work hard, pray harder, and if you have any worries, take them to God—and leave them there.

GUARD YOUR HEART AGAINST ADDICTION

Be sober! Be on the alert!
Your adversary the Devil is prowling around like a roaring lion,
looking for anyone he can devour.

1 Peter 5:8 Holman CSB

We know that we should guard our hearts against the perils of addiction, but we live in a society that often glamorizes the use of drugs, alcohol, cigarettes, and other addictive substances. Why? The answer can be summed up in one word: money. Simply put, addictive substances are big money makers, so suppliers (of both legal and illegal substances) work overtime to make certain that people like you sample their products. The suppliers need a steady stream of new customers because the old ones are dying off (fast), so they engage in a no-holds-barred struggle to find new users—or more accurately, new abusers.

The dictionary defines addiction as "the compulsive need for a habit-forming substance; the condition of being habitually and compulsively occupied with something." That definition

is accurate, but incomplete. For Christians, addiction has
an additional meaning: it means compulsively worshipping
something other than God.

Unless you're living on a deserted island, you know people
who are full-blown addicts—probably lots of people. If you,
or someone you love, is suffering from the blight of addiction,
remember this: Help is available. Plenty of people have
experienced addiction and lived to tell about it . . . so don't give
up hope.

And if you're one of those fortunate people who
hasn't started experimenting with addictive substances,
congratulations! You have just spared yourself a lifetime of
headaches and heartaches.

*Yet in all these things we are more than conquerors
through Him who loved us.*

Romans 8:37 NKJV

A TIP FOR GUARDING YOUR HEART

When it comes to the trap of addiction . . . it's easier to stay
out than it is to get out.

WORDS OF WISDOM

We are meant to be addicted to God, but we develop secondary addictions that temporarily appear to fix our problem.

Edward M. Berckman

It all starts in the mind and the mouth and springs from a lack of balance and self-discipline.

Joyce Meyer

The soul that journeys to God, but doesn't shake off its cares and quiet its appetites, is like someone who drags a cart uphill.

St. John of the Cross

Above all, we must be especially alert against the beginnings of temptation, for the enemy is more easily conquered if he is refused admittance to the mind and is met beyond the threshold when he knocks.

Thomas à Kempis

Addiction is the most powerful psychic enemy of humanity's desire for God.

Gerald May

GOD'S WORDS OF WISDOM

For we do not have a High Priest who cannot sympathize with our weaknesses, but was in all points tempted as we are, yet without sin. Let us therefore come boldly to the throne of grace, that we may obtain mercy and find grace to help in time of need.

Hebrews 4:15-16 NKJV

Jesus responded, "I assure you: Everyone who commits sin is a slave of sin."

John 8:34 Holman CSB

Therefore submit to God. Resist the devil and he will flee from you. Draw near to God and He will draw near to you. Cleanse your hands, you sinners; and purify your hearts, you double-minded.

James 4:7-8 NKJV

Death is the reward of an undisciplined life; your foolish decisions trap you in a dead end.

Proverbs 5:23 MSG

SUMMING IT UP

Guard your heart against addiction . . . or else.

GUARD YOUR HEART AGAINST DISCONTENTMENT

I have learned to be content whatever the circumstances.

Philippians 4:11 NIV

Everywhere we turn, or so it seems, the world promises us contentment and happiness. But the contentment that the world offers is fleeting and incomplete. Thankfully, the contentment that God offers is all encompassing and everlasting.

Happiness depends less upon our circumstances than upon our thoughts. When we turn our thoughts to God, to His gifts, and to His glorious creation, we experience the joy that God intends for His children. But, when we focus on the negative aspects of life—or when we disobey God's commandments—we cause ourselves needless suffering.

Do you sincerely want to be a contented Christian? Then set your mind and your heart upon God's love and His grace. The fullness of life in Christ is available to all who seek it and claim it. Count yourself among that number. Seek first the salvation that is available through a personal relationship with

Jesus Christ, and then claim the joy, the contentment, and the spiritual abundance that the Shepherd offers His sheep.

Let your conduct be without covetousness;
be content with such things as you have.
For He Himself has said,
"I will never leave you nor forsake you."

Hebrews 13:5 NKJV

A TIP FOR GUARDING YOUR HEART

Be contented where you are, even if it's not exactly where you want to end up. God has something wonderful in store for you—and remember that God's timing is perfect—so be patient, trust God, do your best, and expect the best.

WORDS OF WISDOM

When we do what is right, we have contentment, peace, and happiness.

Beverly LaHaye

We are made for God, and nothing less will really satisfy us.

Brennan Manning

The secret of contentment in the midst of change is found in having roots in the changeless Christ—the same yesterday, today and forever.

Ed Young

God is most glorified in us when we are most satisfied in him.

John Piper

Contentment has a way of quieting insatiable desires.

Mary Hunt

GOD'S WORDS OF WISDOM

How priceless is your unfailing love! Both high and low among men find refuge in the shadow of your wings. They feast on the abundance of your house; you give them drink from your river of delights. For with you is the fountain of life; in your light we see light.

Psalm 36:7-9 NIV

The LORD gives strength to his people; the LORD blesses his people with peace.

Psalm 29:11 NIV

Serving God does make us very rich, if we are satisfied with what we have. We brought nothing into the world, so we can take nothing out. But, if we have food and clothes, we will be satisfied with that.

1 Timothy 6:6–8 NCV

A tranquil heart is life to the body, but jealousy is rottenness to the bones.

Proverbs 14:30 Holman CSB

SUMMING IT UP

God offers you His peace, His protection, and His promises. If you accept these gifts, you will be content.

GUARD YOUR HEART WITH GOD'S PROMISES

God also bound himself with an oath, so that those who received the promise could be perfectly sure that he would never change his mind. So God has given us both his promise and his oath. These two things are unchangeable because it is impossible for God to lie. Therefore, we who have fled to him for refuge can take new courage, for we can hold on to his promise with confidence.

Hebrews 6:17-18 NLT

You can guard your heart by standing on the promises of God. And that's precisely what you should do.

What do you expect from the day ahead? Are you willing to trust God completely or are you living beneath a cloud of doubt and fear? God's Word makes it clear: you should trust Him and His promises, and when you do, you can live courageously.

For thoughtful Christians, every day begins and ends with God's Son and God's promises. When we accept Christ into our hearts, God promises us the opportunity for earthy peace and spiritual abundance. But more importantly, God promises us the priceless gift of eternal life.

Sometimes, especially when we find ourselves caught in the inevitable entanglements of life, we fail to trust God completely.

Are you tired? Discouraged? Fearful? Be comforted and trust the promises that God has made to you. Are you worried or anxious? Be confident in God's power. Do you see a difficult future ahead? Be courageous and call upon God. He will protect you and then use you according to His purposes. Are you confused? Listen to the quiet voice of your Heavenly Father. He is not a God of confusion. Talk with Him; listen to Him; trust Him, and trust His promises. He is steadfast, and He is your Protector . . . forever.

Sustain me as You promised, and I will live;
do not let me be ashamed of my hope.

Psalm 119:116 Holman CSB

A TIP FOR GUARDING YOUR HEART

Do you really trust God's promises, or are you hedging your bets? Today, think about the role that God's Word plays in your life, and think about ways that you can worry less and trust God more.

WORDS OF WISDOM

God's promises are medicine for the broken heart. Let Him comfort you. And, after He has comforted you, try to share that comfort with somebody else. It will do both of you good.

Warren Wiersbe

Never doubt in the dark what God told you in the light.

V. Raymond Edman

The meaning of hope isn't just some flimsy wishing. It's a firm confidence in God's promises—that he will ultimately set things right.

Sheila Walsh

We can have full confidence in God's promises because we can have full faith in His character.

Franklin Graham

Faith is confidence in the promises of God or confidence that God will do what He has promised.

Charles Stanley

GOD'S WORDS OF WISDOM

*Patient endurance is what you need now, so you will continue to do
God's will. Then you will receive all that he has promised.*

Hebrews 10:36 NLT

*As for God, his way is perfect. All the LORD's promises prove true.
He is a shield for all who look to him for protection.*

Psalm 18:30 NLT

*Whatever God has promised gets stamped with the Yes of Jesus. In
him, this is what we preach and pray, the great Amen, God's Yes and
our Yes together, gloriously evident.*

2 Corinthians 1:20 MSG

*Let us hold on to the confession of our hope without wavering, for He
who promised is faithful.*

Hebrews 10:23 Holman CSB

SUMMING IT UP

God will most certainly keep His promises to you. Your job is
to keep your obligations to Him.

GUARD YOUR HEART BY COUNTING YOUR BLESSINGS

Blessings are on the head of the righteous.

Proverbs 10:6 Holman CSB

I f you sat down and began counting your blessings, how long would it take? A very, very long time. Your blessings include life, freedom, family, friends, talents, and possessions, for starters. But, your greatest blessing—a gift that is yours for the asking—is God's gift of salvation through Christ Jesus.

Are you a thankful believer who takes time each day to take a partial inventory of the gifts God has given you? Hopefully you are that kind of Christian. After all, God's Word makes it clear: a wise heart is a thankful heart.

We honor God, in part, by the genuine gratitude we feel in our hearts for the blessings He has bestowed upon us. Yet even the most saintly among us must endure periods of fear, doubt, and regret. Why? Because we are imperfect human beings who are incapable of perfect gratitude. Still, even on life's darker days, we must seek to cleanse our hearts of negative emotions and fill them, instead, with praise, with love, with hope, and with thanksgiving. To do otherwise is to be unfair to ourselves, to our loved ones, and to our God.

Sometimes, life-here-on-earth can be complicated, demanding, and frustrating. When the demands of life leave us rushing from place to place with scarcely a moment to spare, we may fail to pause and thank our Creator for His gifts. But, whenever we neglect to give proper thanks to the Father, we suffer because of our misplaced priorities.

Today, begin making a list of your blessings. You most certainly will not be able to make a complete list, but take a few moments and jot down as many blessings as you can. Then, give thanks to the Giver of all good things: God. His love for you is eternal, as are His gifts. And it's never too soon—or too late—to offer Him thanks.

*Unfailing love surrounds those who trust the L*ORD.

Psalm 32:10 NLT

A TIP FOR GUARDING YOUR HEART

Carve out time to thank God for His blessings. Take time out of every day (not just on Sundays) to praise God and thank Him for His gifts.

WORDS OF WISDOM

God is always far more willing to give us good things than we are anxious to have them.

Catherine Marshall

It is when we give ourselves to be a blessing that we can specially count on the blessing of God.

Andrew Murray

With the goodness of God to desire our highest welfare and the wisdom of God to plan it, what do we lack? Surely we are the most favored of all creatures.

A. W. Tozer

God's love for His children is unconditional, no strings attached. But, God's blessings on our lives do come with a condition— obedience. If we are to receive the fullness of God's blessings, we must obey Him and keep His commandments.

Jim Gallery

The Christian life is motivated, not by a list of do's and don'ts, but by the gracious outpouring of God's love and blessing.

Anne Graham Lotz

GOD'S WORDS OF WISDOM

You will show me the path of life; in Your presence is fullness of joy;
at Your right hand are pleasures forevermore.

Psalm 16:11 NKJV

For surely, O Lord, you bless the righteous; you surround them with
your favor as with a shield.

Psalm 5:12 NIV

The Lord is kind and merciful, slow to get angry, full of unfailing
love. The Lord is good to everyone. He showers compassion on all his
creation.

Psalm 145:8-9 NLT

Blessed is a man who endures trials, because when he passes the test
he will receive the crown of life that He has promised to those who
love Him.

James 1:12 Holman CSB

SUMMING IT UP

God has given you more blessings than you can count. Your
job is to accept them and be grateful.

GUARD YOUR HEART WITH KNOWLEDGE

Get all the advice and instruction you can,
and be wise the rest of your life.

Proverbs 19:20 NLT

Whether you're twenty-two or a hundred and two, you've still got lots to learn. Even if you're very wise, God isn't finished with you yet, and He isn't finished teaching you important lessons about life here on earth and life eternal.

God does not intend for you to be a stagnant believer. Far from it! God wants you to continue growing as a person and as a Christian every day that you live. And make no mistake: both spiritual and intellectual growth are possible during every stage of life.

Are you a curious Christian who has committed yourself to the regimen of regular Bible study, or do you consult your Bible on a hit-or-miss basis? The answer to this question will be an indication of the extent to which you allow God to direct the course of your life.

As a spiritual being, you have the potential to grow in your personal knowledge of the Lord every day that you live. You can do so through prayer, through worship, through an openness to

God's Holy Spirit, and through a careful study of God's Holy Word. Your Bible contains powerful prescriptions for everyday living. If you sincerely seek to walk with God, you should commit yourself to the thoughtful study of His teachings.

Do you seek to live a life of righteousness and wisdom? If so, you must continue to study the ultimate source of wisdom: the Word of God. You must associate, day in and day out, with godly men and women. And, you must act in accordance with your beliefs.

When you study God's Word and live according to His commandments, you will become wise . . . and you will serve as a shining example to your friends, to you family, and to the world.

*Remember what you are taught,
and listen carefully to words of knowledge.*

Proverbs 23:12 NCV

A TIP FOR GUARDING YOUR HEART

Your future depends, to a very great extent, upon how much you are willing to invest in yourself. So keep learning and keep growing personally, professionally, and spiritually.

WORDS OF WISDOM

True learning can take place at every age of life, and it doesn't have to be in the curriculum plan.

Suzanne Dale Ezell

While chastening is always difficult, if we look to God for the lesson we should learn, we will see spiritual fruit.

Vonette Bright

The wonderful thing about God's schoolroom is that we get to grade our own papers. You see, He doesn't test us so He can learn how well we're doing. He tests us so we can discover how well we're doing.

Charles Swindoll

The wise man gives proper appreciation in his life to this past. He learns to sift the sawdust of heritage in order to find the nuggets that make the current moment have any meaning.

Grady Nutt

It's the things you learn after you know it all that really count.

Vance Havner

GOD'S WORDS OF WISDOM

The fear of the Lord is the beginning of knowledge, but fools despise wisdom and discipline.

Proverbs 1:7 NIV

The knowledge of the secrets of the kingdom of heaven has been given to you . . . .

Matthew 13:11 NIV

For now we see indistinctly, as in a mirror, but then face to face. Now I know in part, but then I will know fully, as I am fully known.

1 Corinthians 13:12 Holman CSB

Now if any of you lacks wisdom, he should ask God, who gives to all generously and without criticizing, and it will be given to him.

James 1:5 Holman CSB

SUMMING IT UP

God still has important lessons to teach you. Your task is to be open to His instruction.

GUARD YOUR HEART BY ACCEPTING GOD'S PEACE

The peace of God, which surpasses all understanding,
will guard your hearts and minds through Christ Jesus.

Philippians 4:7 NKJV

Have you found the lasting peace that can—and should—be yours through Jesus Christ? Or are you still chasing the illusion of "peace and happiness" that the world promises but cannot deliver?

The beautiful words of John 14:27 promise that Jesus offers peace, not as the world gives, but as He alone gives: "Peace I leave with you. My peace I give to you. I do not give to you as the world gives. Your heart must not be troubled or fearful" (Holman CSB). Your challenge is to accept Christ's peace into your heart and then, as best you can, to share His peace with your neighbors. But sometimes, that's easier said than done.

If you are a person with lots of obligations and plenty of responsibilities, it is simply a fact of life: You worry. From time to time, you worry about finances, safety, health, home, family, or about countless other concerns, some great and some small.

Where is the best place to take your worries? Take them to God . . . and leave them there.

The Scottish preacher George McDonald observed, "It has been well said that no man ever sank under the burden of the day. It is when tomorrow's burden is added to the burden of today that the weight is more than a man can bear. Never load yourselves so, my friends. If you find yourselves so loaded, at least remember this: it is your own doing, not God's. He begs you to leave the future to Him."

Today, as a gift to yourself, to your family, and to your friends, claim the inner peace that is your spiritual birthright: the peace of Jesus Christ. Christ is standing at the door, waiting patiently for you to invite Him to reign over your heart. His eternal peace is offered freely. Claim it today.

Come to terms with God and be at peace;
in this way good will come to you.

Job 22:21 Holman CSB

A TIP FOR GUARDING YOUR HEART

Do you want to discover God's peace? Then do your best to live in the center of God's will.

WORDS OF WISDOM

In the center of a hurricane there is absolute quiet and peace.
There is no safer place than in the center of the will of God.

Corrie ten Boom

I believe that in every time and place it is within our power to
acquiesce in the will of God—and what peace it brings to do so!

Elisabeth Elliot

There may be no trumpet sound or loud applause when we make
a right decision, just a calm sense of resolution and peace.

Gloria Gaither

God loves you and wants you to experience peace and life—
abundant and eternal.

Billy Graham

A great many people are trying to make peace, but that has
already been done. God has not left it for us to do; all we have
to do is to enter into it.

D. L. Moody

GOD'S WORDS OF WISDOM

God has called us to live in peace.

1 Corinthians 7:15 NIV

And let the peace of God rule in your hearts . . . and be ye thankful.

Colossians 3:15 KJV

You will keep in perfect peace him whose mind is steadfast, because he trusts in you.

Isaiah 26:3 NIV

I have told you these things, so that in me you may have peace. In this world you will have trouble. But take heart! I have overcome the world.

John 16:33 NIV

But now in Christ Jesus, you who were far away have been brought near by the blood of the Messiah. For He is our peace, who made both groups one and tore down the dividing wall of hostility.

Ephesians 2:13-14 Holman CSB

SUMMING IT UP

God's peace surpasses human understanding. When you accept His peace, it will revolutionize your life.

ABOVE ALL ELSE: YOUR RELATIONSHIP WITH CHRIST

I assure you, anyone who believes in me already has eternal life.

John 6:47 NLT

How marvelous it is that God became a man and walked among us. Had He not chosen to do so, we might feel removed from a distant Creator. But ours is not a distant God. Ours is a God who understands—far better than we ever could—the essence of what it means to be human.

God understands our hopes, our fears, and our temptations. He understands what it means to be angry and what it costs to forgive. He knows the heart, the conscience, and the soul of every person who has ever lived, including you. And God has a plan of salvation that is intended for you. Accept it. Accept God's gift through the person of His Son Christ Jesus, and then rest assured: God walked among us so that you might have eternal life; amazing though it may seem, He did it for you.

As mere mortals, our vision for the future, like our lives here on earth, is limited. God's vision is not burdened by such limitations: His plans extend throughout all eternity. Thus,

God's plans for you are not limited to the ups and downs of everyday life. Your Heavenly Father has bigger things in mind . . . much bigger things.

Let us praise the Creator for His priceless gift, and let us share the Good News with all who cross our paths. We return our Father's love by accepting His grace and by sharing His message and His love. When we do, we are blessed here on earth and throughout all eternity.

As you struggle with the inevitable hardships and occasional disappointments of life, remember that God has invited you to accept His abundance not only for today but also for all eternity. So keep things in perspective. Although you will inevitably encounter occasional defeats in this world, you'll have all eternity to celebrate the ultimate victory in the next.

These things I have written to you who believe
in the name of the Son of God,
that you may know that you have eternal life.

1 John 5:13 NKJV

A Tip for Guarding Your Heart

Your eternity with God is secure when you believe in Jesus.

WORDS OF WISDOM

He who has no vision of eternity will never get a true hold of time.

Thomas Carlyle

Life: the time God gives you to determine how you spend eternity.

Anonymous

We'll spend eternity exploring and rejoicing in the unsearchable riches of God's character, purpose, love, Living Word, and astounding creativity.

Susan Lenzkes

Live near to God, and all things will appear little to you in comparison with eternal realities.

Robert Murray McCheyne

This short, earthly life, important and significant though it may be in its setting, is no more than a prelude to a share in the timeless Life of God.

J. B. Phillips

GOD'S WORDS OF WISDOM

And this is the testimony: that God has given us eternal life, and this life is in His Son. He who has the Son has life; he who does not have the Son of God does not have life.

1 John 5:11-12 NKJV

Don't be troubled. You trust God, now trust in me. There are many rooms in my Father's home, and I am going to prepare a place for you. If this were not so, I would tell you plainly. When everything is ready, I will come and get you, so that you will always be with me where I am.

John 14:1-3 NLT

Pursue righteousness, godliness, faith, love, endurance, and gentleness. Fight the good fight for the faith; take hold of eternal life, to which you were called and have made a good confession before many witnesses.

1 Timothy 6:11-12 Holman CSB

Jesus said to her, "I am the resurrection and the life. The one who believes in Me, even if he dies, will live. Everyone who lives and believes in Me will never die—ever. Do you believe this?"

John 11:25-26 Holman CSB

SUMMING IT UP

God offers you life abundant and life eternal. Accept His gift today.

Above all else, guard your heart, for it affects everything you do. Avoid all perverse talk; stay far from corrupt speech. Look straight ahead, and fix your eyes on what lies before you. Mark out a straight path for your feet; then stick to the path and stay safe. Don't get sidetracked; keep your feet from following evil.

Proverbs 4:23-27 NLT

Tim Way has been on staff with Family Christian Stores for the past twenty three years. He is currently the Senior Buyer of Book, Bibles and Church Resources. Tim and his wife, Ramona, live in Grand Rapids, Michigan. They have three grown children and three grandchildren.

Dr. Criswell Freeman is a best-selling author with over 14,000,000 books in print. He is a graduate of Vanderbilt University. He received his doctoral degree from the Adler School of Professional Psychology in Chicago; he also attended classes at Southern Seminary in Louisville where he was mentored by the late Wayne Oates, a pioneer in the field of pastoral counseling. Dr. Freeman is married; he has two children.